WOUNDED WORLD
AND
BROKEN CHURCH

For Kathleen

SERMONS
TOWARD HEALING

WOUNDED WORLD AND BROKEN CHURCH

— KEITH ROWE —

COVENTRY PRESS

Published in Australia by
Coventry Press
33 Scoresby Road
Bayswater VIC 3153

ISBN 9781922589231

Copyright © Keith Rowe 2022

All rights reserved. Other than for the purposes and subject to the conditions prescribed under the *Copyright Act*, no part of this publication may be reproduced, stored in a retrieval system, or transmitted in any form or by any means, electronic, mechanical, photocopying, recording or otherwise, without the prior permission of the publisher.

Scripture quotations are from the *New Revised Standard Version Bible*, copyright 1989, Division of Christian Education of the National Council of the Churches of Christ in the United States of America. Used by permission. All rights reserved.

Catalogue-in-Publication entry is available from the National Library of Australia
http://catalogue.nla.gov.au

Cover design by Ian James – www.jgd.com.au
Text design by Coventry Press
Set in EB Garamond

Printed in Australia

Contents

Introduction		9
A wounded church in a wounded world		**13**
1.	'Psalm 88 and a wintry spirituality'	15
2.	Do you worry about the future of the church? John 3:1-10	21
3.	When temples fall Mark 13:1-8	25
4.	What happened to the good news? Mark 1:14-20	31
5.	Remembering St Francis while Assembly meets	37
6.	The adventures of church table 1 Corinthians 11:17-22	43
7.	Orientation to a new congregation	49
Rediscovering Jesus and the way he pioneered		**51**
1.	Who is this man? Matthew 21:1-11	53
2.	Cradles into which Jesus was born Matthew 2:1-12	58

3.	Living in the wilderness in the spirit of Jesus Matthew 4:1-11	65
4.	Jesus' homecoming sermon Luke 4:16-30	71

Building the way, on the way — 77

1.	Jesus converted by a Canaanite woman Matthew 15: 21-28	79
2.	A world without scapegoats? Luke 9:51-62	85
3.	The prophet and the centurion Luke 7:1-10	91
4.	A prophet of the new order Luke 7:36-50	97

Stewards of the way pioneered by Jesus — 103

1.	Stewards of the words of Jesus John 17:8	105
2.	Refusing to serve an unjust system Matthew 25:14-30	112
3.	A moment of grace for the prodigal family Luke 15:11-32	120
4.	The rich man and Lazarus Luke 16:19-31	126
5.	Human greed and a world suffering the effects Luke 19:1-10, Matthew 6:24	132
6.	Neighbours! Luke 10:25-37	139

7.	Good Samaritan? You've got to be kidding! Luke 10:25-37; John 4:3-26	145
8.	Good seed, poor soils and God-grace Genesis 25:19-34; Matthew 13:1-9, 18-23	152
9.	Good news, bad news Matthew 20:1-16	157
10.	Fishing nets, God-love and a needy world Matthew 4:12-23	163

Protect the wall or plant the seeds?   **169**

1.	Rediscovering the adventure Mark 1:1-14	173
2.	Sabbath discipline and the maintenance of identity Mark 2:23 to 3:6	178
3.	Naming Jesus and doing Jesus Mark 8:27-38	185
4.	For which all else is expendable Mark 9:42-50; Luke 4:14-21	191

About the author   198

Introduction

To publish a book of sermons may assume an overly optimistic assessment of contemporary reading habits. There was a time when collections of sermons were top sellers but alas...

By their very nature, sermons are occasional pieces, spoken explorations of important matters in the context of Christian worship and followed by conversation with those who want to challenge and/or build on what has been said. During retirement years, I have twice found myself worshipping in a Christian congregation without an ordained Minister and have been invited to become once again a preacher and liturgist. I've enjoyed the experience – a disciplined opportunity to keep on working at issues of Christian belief and practice and an opportunity to share emerging and lasting convictions – whatever I have discovered or am discovering – with others.

A number of people urged me to publish a book of sermons but I was diffident, feeling that a preacher's words belong within the community within which they were shared. Neville Watson, a most remarkable Christian man, from Wembley Downs in Perth, Western Australia, refused to accept my diffidence and persisted till I agreed to gather this selection of sermons and part sermons in the hope they might be of interest and assistance to others within the broader Christian community.

There is something unfinished, incomplete, about each of these sermons and part sermons. Sometimes they leave as many questions as they provide answers. As I thought about this apparent problem I recognised afresh – what I'm often aware of in the act of preaching – that incompleteness is a desired element in effective preaching. The act of preaching should tease hearers into further and deepening exploration into their own believing, living and ways of being church, of contributing to the healing of our broken world, of fulfilling the promise of their humanity. I hope these sermons and excerpts from sermons will do that for you. They need to be completed, amplified, given life by their readers.

I would like to encourage those who have become disenchanted with churchy versions of Christian believing and living that are no longer credible or who are trapped into churchly roles they feel requires then to give assent to ancient convictions they no longer agree with. Perhaps they can no longer accept the tragic and damaging claim that the church alone (or a particular version of church!) has access to truth.

They will certainly be pained when they hear pernicious and life-denying claims that 'God' sends suffering, pandemic, cyclones and tragedy to individuals and nations as divine punishment for whatever offends the speaker. It is no wonder that views like these cause reasonable and compassionate people to give up on the church. I hope that what I have written will be helpful to readers who seek a thoughtful, spiritually and socially sensitive approach to Christian believing, those who, while remaining within the church family, are disenchanted, even disgusted, with the dogmatism, obscurantism and judgmental attitudes that characterise too many congregations and 'Christian' organisations. The Christian gospel is bigger than that: more generous, more thoughtful, more interesting, less defensive, more open to life and to a just and peaceable future, more open to adventure.

If everyone is to have a 'label', then I certainly sit within the 'Progressive Christian' way of thinking and living. By Progressive Christianity, I mean a contemporary form of Christian existence that has deep roots in the Christian tradition and seeks to contribute to the renewal of the Christian way and the human adventure through rethinking Christian belief and practice in the light of insights and understandings not available to earlier generations and to the renewal of Christian living through recapturing the radical social implications of the way of life explored by Jesus.

Preaching is a form of thoughtful conversation without footnotes but in this written form I have added some suggestions for further explorations, named a few books, to assist those who might want to follow ideas, hunches or suggestions made by me but dependant on the wisdom and scholarship of others. There are many forms and styles of preaching, different starting points and many ways of sharing, in fragile human words, the Way pioneered by Jesus. In the congregations where these sermons were preached, I was one of a number of preachers and liturgists and this enabled differing styles of presentation and conviction to complement one another.

Since student days, I have been saddened by the great gap existing between the important and thoughtful work of theologians and Biblical scholars on the one hand and what is presented in our pulpits and shared with the folks in the pews. Over the years and in a number of settings, I have sought to share and publicly explore the wisdom of the scholarly and thoughtful section of the Christian family – both past and present – and to encourage conversation and mutual exploration between Gospel wisdom and scientific, historical, economic and social knowledge. I look forward to a time when the church – or whatever replaces church as we have experienced it – becomes a genuine community of explorers and thoughtful participants in the way pioneered by Jesus.

There's another gap or closed door in the life of most churches. This is the gap between challenging words spoken in the pulpit or prayed at the prayer desk and decisions made in Parish Council or whatever group plans and nurtures what is usually described as the 'mission' of the church, the things this group of friends does in response to its exploration of the way pioneered by Jesus, their contribution to the healing of the world, their presence in a particular community. Pulpit or study group exploration of the Way pioneered by Jesus and hints as to what they might mean in our time, words spoken with much thought and sensitivity to the purposes of God made clear in Jesus, are mislaid in the short walk from pews, pulpit and prayer desk to the meeting room and so called 'business agendas'.

Attending to denominational housekeeping, leaking downpipes and clergy leave provisions seem to take precedence over the hard thinking, careful planning and courageous action involved in exploring what and how it means to live the Way pioneered by Jesus. It's a gap that should trouble us

I hope these sermonic explorations might offer a little light in what is a dark time for the Christian adventure. It's an even darker time for humanity and for our fragile planet. Climate change and environmental destruction, the continuing and growing gap between rich and poor, possibilities and perils in the development of 'artificial intelligence' and fresh awareness of human fragility revealed during covid pandemic times all cry out for fresh thinking and bold action. These and other challenges are the setting of our believing, praying and living.

Some themes and ideas are repeated in more than one sermon. I've not sought to avoid this apparent replication. Rather, it reflects that these sermons were preached over a period of years and means the integrity of the original sermon – as a response to the promise inherent in a Biblical text – is retained.

In a second volume, I explore – again through sermons – the nature of interfaith dialogue and shared action and how we may speak of God in a 'no god' world.

Keith Rowe

A WOUNDED CHURCH IN A WOUNDED WORLD

When, in 1963, I was appointed to my first parish charge, New Zealand society still bore the marks of churchly influence. At the very least, people knew what church they no longer attended, they had a nodding acquaintance with biblical stories and in times of need sought help from their Minister or Priest. Sixty years later, the scene has changed radically. Census returns suggest that about half of those responding to a question about religious allegiance describe themselves as being without any religion and this response has grown dramatically over recent decades. Of course, we don't know exactly what this response means in personal terms or whether it's a response shaped by careful thought. There are more ways of being 'religious' than what churches, mosques and temples represent. The census form does not offer Free Market Capitalism, Sport or Nationalism as other 'religious' possibilities. Nor is it clear exactly what it means to tick the box of a named Christian denomination. However, the bottom line reality for those who care about the Way of life embodied by Jesus is clear: the organisation responsible for promoting the Way he pioneered is no longer seen as credible, needed, or worth being part of by a growing number of people.

1

'Psalm 88 and a wintry spirituality'

> How do we describe our times? It feels like the church is experiencing a wintry period in its journey through human history. Many of us remember the church's summer times – a place in the sun, busy programs, on a respected rung in the social pecking order, its leaders heeded by politicians and decision-makers, a time when Biblical stories and insights were known and respected. Where and when did the summer end? Will the spring return and how will we recognise its coming? This sermon was, of course, preached as winter began to impose its icy grip on our community but the sentiment and the reality are true for societies, individuals and organisations, whatever the temperature.

There's no doubt we're held firmly in the grip of winter. It seemed to creep up on us this year without the normal autumnal warnings. All of a sudden, it seemed, a prolonged warm summer was blown away and replaced by wind, rain and cold. In other parts of the country snow, flood and storm became reminders of just how tough winter can be. You've just got to sit it out in the confidence that spring will come with the same stealth; and summer will eventually return. But in the meantime, it's warm coats, head colds and extra blankets.

Over the last few weeks, I've reread a 1983 book by noted Christian historian and commentator, Martin Marty of Chicago, *A cry of absence, reflections for the winter of the heart*. Marty's a wise and sensitive man and always has something of enduring value to share. He begins with reference to words of a great twentieth century theologian, Karl Rahner. Rahner, by then an old man, in reflecting on life describes two forms of Christian spirituality – 'summer spirituality' and 'wintry spirituality'. Summer spirituality bathes in the warm immediacy of God's ever-present and personalised love. Joy, happiness, optimism, confidence and certainty abound. Bad times may come but they're easily discounted as temporary blips on life's summery radar. Rahner identifies Pentecostalism and the charismatic movement as contemporary expressions of summery spirituality.

Wintery spirituality, on the other hand, senses more acutely the shadow and struggle side of life. Grief, doubt, ignorance, pain, loneliness and despair are also part of life and clamour for attention. Christian belief may be held more tentatively and, critically, remaining open to amendment as life unfolds and the storms of life cause one to reflect yet again on what it all means. If summery believers seem to over-believe, Rahner (referring doubtless to his own experience) suggests that wintry believers often find common cause with unbelievers who similarly acknowledge the ambiguities and puzzling aspects of human existence. Asked which type the church should give preference to, Rahner claims both are needed but then suggests that the church should not place all its hopes in the summery expression of Christian life. The church 'has to think more than it has previously done about how to frame the message for people who are troubled, but who in the end have a faith which is certainly not strengthened by a spirituality of the charismatic type'.

In his book, Martin Marty re-reads some of the wintry psalms – psalms like Psalm 88, (see also 90 and 39). I was not surprised to discover Psalm 88 is not included in the church's three-year lectionary of psalms to be read at Sunday worship. Is it too stark, too much touched by winter experience, naming experiences or possibilities we'd prefer to skip over? The themes of aloneness, lostness, shut in a pit, sorrow, darkness, dead and despair recur. Other psalms like this end with a benediction at the end, an affirmation that God is God and we'll be OK in the end. Nothing like that here!

The last word of the psalm is 'darkness'. Marty wrote his book in the shadow period following the death of his wife from cancer. During a period of chemotherapy treatment, he and his wife took daily turns at reading the psalms. He read the even numbers and she the odd. When they reached Psalm 88, with its wintry acknowledgment of tough times, he suggested to his wife she was in no state to hear such wintry sentiments. She urged him to read it, claiming 'we need these down psalms, the dark ones, otherwise the joyful psalms, the hallelujah ones, won't touch our lives'. Marty reflects: 'I have learned in dealing with people that a spiritual life devoted entirely to highs and happiness and 'praise the Lord' simply doesn't do justice to reality, including Biblical reality and the most profound Jewish and Christian spirituality'.

It must surely be a sign of emerging adulthood when we first recognise that life is not, and will never be, a simple, warm summer walk down a petal-strewn pathway of never-ending bliss. Hopefully, we can recall summery times when life flowed calmly and in fulfilling paths. We should cherish such times and welcome them as gifts to be treasured. But winter winds will surely come, often when we least expect them. The death of loved ones means that lingering grief casts its sad shadow even when the sun is shining for others. Many of us know the hollow feeling that never fully heals but we somehow learn to live with. Failure, disappointments, unrealised hopes and dreams, broken friendships – all bring their own wintry moods and questions. We joke about the milestone that is retirement with its hoped for release from deadlines, demands and discipline but even the word 'retirement' can take on a somewhat wintry aspect with its undertones of 'no longer needed', 'past your best', 'in the waiting room' and so on.

Over recent centuries. a distinctive and somewhat wintry expression of Christian faith and belief has been born. Karl Rahner wrote that, as children of the post-enlightenment West (a period in western history when doubt became valued and experience took precedence over tradition), we've inherited a more wintry kind of spirituality. In a sense, if we are thoughtful and sensitive to our times, we cannot escape from it. We bring to the altar of faith not only affirmations but also doubts, questions and hesitations. We no longer live in a society shaped by officially sanctioned and universally understood Christianity. We must now give good reasons for the faith and hope that is in us. We've learned, or are learning, to find truth in other places and among other people than our ancestors did. The claims we make for the church and for Christ are typically more modest than those held by our great grandparents.

A deeper, more realistic, compassionate and robust form of Christian faith is being born in our time – one as much at home in winter winds as in summer sun, open to life's tough questions, not flinching from challenges brought by a secular distrust of religion, trusting 'God' even when we lack words to describe what we most deeply believe. Too much popular Christianity is winter denying. That's why, I think, people who in the sunny days of adolescence and young adulthood find meaning and pleasure in Pentecostal or fundamentalist forms of Christianity, later give it all away when they encounter life's winter periods and find themselves unable to function in the absence of sunshine.

'Psalm 88 and a wintry spirituality'

The sunny side of my disposition wants to hurry on to spring, assuring myself that winter always passes and nature returns to the enervating, fertile and relaxing rhythms of summer. Marty reminded me that in real life the sun does not always reappear. Winter is a time of preparation for the coming of spring but it's also a time of death for many creatures. Some things don't ever fully heal. Life does not always provide happy endings. For every person released from the clutches of ill health, many more succumb to the ravages of a damaged body. I'm not trying to be gloomy. I'm standing within the tradition of the wintry psalms and their refusal to let us fool ourselves into believing that somehow we're bullet proof and we dwell in unceasing and ever returning sunshine.

In a community where wintry times are acknowledged, we have the opportunity of supporting and encouraging one another when winter winds blow. In the last parish of which we were part, collectively we went through a painful winter period before and following the death of a much loved Minister. We made it through that cold winter time because we held one another, said our prayers together and continued to believe that held within Spirit we would eventually welcome more summery days. We became a better people, a stronger community, because we walked together through winter winds.

Some suggest the Christian church has entered into a wintery and wandering period in its life. There's no turning back to ancient securities. The attempt to chart a pathway through the uncertainties of today require more than a rediscovery of creeds, dogmas and structures better suited to earlier times and places. The nearest biblical period to our times may be the period of exile when the Israelite people lived as semi-prisoners in Babylon, far away from their ancient securities and life-enhancing customs. They learned a new way of being the People of God during the winter of their exile. They gathered stories of faith that could sustain them over the long haul, They discovered new ways of being the People of God. Winter's a time when soil is prepared for planting and when we pray and plan a pathway toward spring's new shoots and beyond to summer fruit.

A last word from Martin Marty. Referring to the wintry mood of psalm 88, Marty notes that even in the darkness of pain, alienation and hopelessness the psalmist still addresses God, reaches out to what he describes as a 'steadfast love' that, though not currently experienced, is trusted as final truth. Even in the winter, God is named as the background of meaning and purpose that even in the toughest winter, in ways beyond our understanding, sustains us and enables us to keep going. Amen.

Exploring Further

In addition to Marty's helpful book, there are other writers who reflect on the wintry days of today's church. Some Biblical scholars like Walter Brueggemann describe the contemporary church living in a time of exile akin to that experienced by Israel in the 6th century B.C. when the leadership of the Hebrew community were geographically and spiritually forced to live in another land.

Our exile may not be geographic but, culturally and spiritually, we live in an era when the faith we treasure is no longer valued by the society in which we live. Our lives are shaped by the all-embracing western values of consumerism, accumulation of wealth and a search for power. In *Cadences of Home, preaching among exiles*, (1997), Brueggemann explores how our time in 'exile' can be a time of spiritual and theological rediscovery of the Way of Jesus and of new ways of being a healing presence in a broken world.

2

Do you worry about the future of the church?

John 3:1-10

> I was invited to preach in a small and financially marginal congregation on 'mothering Sunday'. I learned that Mothering Sunday was originally intended to be a day when, in fact or imagination, and, as part of their Lenten preparation for Easter, worshippers would return to the place of their baptism, the place where they were first 'mothered' into the way of Jesus. But is there a church to return to?

According to tradition, this is a Sunday to recall a particular group of people, a place, a building, a place of childhood years perhaps, a Christian community with its own particular way of expressing faith and living life. Some of you may have a memory of the church of your baptism, but it's possible, even likely, that there's no church building remaining or no active community of faith still meeting in that area, for over recent decades the church has been sailing through rough weather. Congregations have closed because of declining numbers, church buildings have become dwellings, restaurants or community centres, the wisdom of the Christian community has become less valued by society and other interests and activities have replaced church. Fewer people seek baptism for their children or, if they do, it has less and less to do with being incorporated into the stream of life pioneered by Jesus.

That's the reality in which we live. As members of the church, we are members of a community living on the margins of society, a little lost, a little shell shocked, wondering what the future holds for the church we have loved and served.

Our Gospel reading brings with it a suggestion that we imagine ourselves to have been 'mothered' in faith by an equally fragile first century community of Jesus followers who valued and sought to live within the Jesus Way as described in the Gospel of John. Beyond the hallowed words of the New Testament there were real people who like us were trying to make sense of life, to live it well, to care for their neighbours and who were convinced that the way of life pioneered by Jesus was important not only for them but for their world.

We know very little for certain about the details of the Johannine communities of faith. It's likely they formed a network of house churches, shaped by the way of life commended by John and his take on the ministry and teaching of Jesus. They thought of Jesus as the lived presence of the breath of God within the human family – the same gentle creative energy that was present at creation and continues to blow through human history. Most members came from a strongly Jewish background and were convinced that the way pioneered by Jesus was the best pathway into an enriched future for the battered Jewish community and for others who wondered whether human life could have meaning and purpose. Nicodemus represents them; schooled as Jews and loyal to the ancient ways yet also attracted to the freshness and simplicity of the way of Jesus. Whatever their background, they were bound together by this life-shaping conviction that Jesus, in his teaching, his actions, his living and dying, was the clue to as to how God intended life to be lived.

There is a beautiful legend about the Christian community in Ephesus, the place where it is believed John died. When John was a very old man he would be brought into the group to give a blessing and he would simply say, 'God is love, love one another'. Just imagine if every Sunday one of the older members of the congregation were, like John, to give the same reminder of what matters most. Perhaps there could be a roster, naming who will give the 'John Reminder' of what we know but often forget.

Since those earliest days, the Christian church has had a chequered history. There have been times of heroic faith but also times when it has been captured by destructive attitudes and behaviours, when it has been more shaped by loyalty to those with power than care for the most needy, times when it has been shaped by attitudes every bit as bad as those displayed by the Roman Empire in the time of Jesus. But there have always been women and men who, like John, have stayed within the central affirmations that 'God is love', that love is the clue, that Jesus embodied and embodies that love within human history and that new beginnings (even as small as mustard seeds!) are always possible.

I wonder, sometimes worry, about what the future holds for the Christian church in places like Australia and New Zealand. Will it survive or in what form will it survive? Can it be born again? Can it start all over or at least shed the worst of the structural and attitudinal hindrances it has picked up over the centuries? Business as usual will not be enough for that's exactly what's not working. I wonder too how we can be 'mother' churches, planting seeds of possibility, from which the future church can be born or mothered. The church may be born again but the form of its life may differ from what we know.

We can do without a lot of what we take for granted – grand buildings, inherited authority structures and a host of outdated customs. There will, I suspect, always be a need for networks of usually small communities of people where the deeds and words of Jesus are remembered, discussed, lived out and shared. I think it's likely that in such communities there will be a shared meal during which Jesus is remembered and when together they act out and pray for ('Your Kingdom come, your will be done') the 'Jesus dream' of a time when all food is shared and all people are united as a single family.

Perhaps the question for us as we think of the future of this and many other congregations is the same as the one faced by the church of John long ago: 'What does it mean, what will it mean, for us and our successors, in weakness and in strength, to keep alive the way of Jesus and to play our part, however modest it may seem, in weaving the way of Jesus into the fabric of our society?' It's a worthwhile question for 'mothering Sunday'.

Exploring Further

> There are many books written from within Protestant and Catholic perspectives that identify the need for dramatic change in structure, doctrine and deed if the church is to endure in any meaningful sense. The predicament has been well analysed. An example is John Shelby Spong, *Why Christianity must change or die*, 1998. Will renewal come from decisions and edicts of Synods, Assemblies or Conferences or will it grow from grass roots courage?

3

When temples fall

Mark 13:1-8

> The Christian movement grew from the destruction of the Jerusalem Temple. It was one of a number of Jewish responses to the question: what will give form and direction to our journey into God-love in the absence of the Temple? Faith continues even after temples fall – or does it wither because it has mistaken loyalty to human structures for what beckons, troubles and energises us, what some called Spirit?

Our reading from Mark 13 is a passage that has cast a negative shadow over the Christian adventure. No sooner has an earthquake, war, tsunami or damaging cyclone touched the earth than ardent and apparently Bible believing people claim that God has sent the disaster, is summoning us to repent of our sins, and that the end of the world is around the next corner. They'd be more believable if the same sad and misguided predictions hadn't been made for hundreds of years. Liberal-progressive Christians tend to leave passages like this to the fundamentalist right wing.

Well, I'm not willing to leave any part of the Bible in the sole ownership of the fundamentalists. The whole Bible belongs to the whole church. I think there's gold in this passage but it's got nothing to do with predicting the end of the world or a violent and judgmental return of Jesus.

The background to our text is the distress and societal upheaval resulting from a long drawn-out Jewish revolt that culminated in the destruction of the Jerusalem temple in AD 70 (forty years after the time of Jesus). This huge structure, employing up to two thousand priests at a time, dominated the city. It was the social, political and economic hub around which Jewish society revolved. Its destruction, that is still lamented in Israel and within the Jewish community, may not have signalled the end of the world in a cosmic sense but it most certainly represented the end of the Jewish world as it was valued and understood at that time. The sense of loss was catastrophic. It was as though God had finally deserted the chosen people and all they held dear was turned to worthless dust. All they thought they had achieved lay in ruins. Every death, every fallen temple stone felt like a 'sign of the end.' The Temple, this was the third to be erected on the site, was regarded as a sign of God's presence within the Jewish community, a living pledge of God's commitment to their wellbeing. And now it was gone. Finish!

Mark's Gospel was written within a few years of these dreadful events. The sense of loss was still fresh among Mark's Jewish Christian readers and hearers. Reflecting on all that had happened, they sensed a linkage between the death of Jesus and the death of the Temple. Each was an event that shattered hope and left behind feelings of anger, puzzlement and despair. How could a building and a person as beautiful and as life enhancing as these be destroyed by human foolishness? So Mark inserted an imaginary conversation between Jesus and his disciples discussing together how they should respond to the events of AD 70. He placed this conversation into his narrative of the journey of Jesus to Jerusalem and before his account of the death of Jesus. So recollection of Jesus and awareness of events in their own time were brought together. There's a suggestion that the death of Jesus was on a par with,

When temples fall Mark 13:1-8

perhaps even more significant for humanity, than the fall of the Temple. Each event marks the end of a world and the beginning of a new cycle in the human journey. It would be fun to follow the fascinating scholarly debates that whirl around the words of Mark 13 but my concern is more with what wisdom these unlikely words might throw on our lives and the life of our current world.

The underlying assumption of the chapter is that change is written into life. The Temple may have served and saved Jewish identity for many years and in successive buildings but no system, no structure, no dogma lasts forever. Jesus is not pictured lamenting the demise of the temple, nor does he welcome this dreadful event. Mark pictures Jesus saying to followers living forty years after his death that this was change they may regret but they have to accept that the world they took for granted was at an end and they must now learn to trust God in new ways as they make their way into a future without familiar signposts or cleared pathways.

Jesus was a visionary. Aware of the shortcomings of the present, he reached toward a future shaped by peace, justice, generosity and hospitality. He sought change in the way people lived and gave shape to their life together. The poor welcomed him because the present was a time of pain and exclusion for them. The wealthy and powerful opposed him for present arrangements served them well and ensured their continuing comfort.

Change is implicit in the message of Jesus. Those of our day for whom Christian discipleship has become a program for resisting change are surely in error. Our task is not to protect and preserve temples, systems, structures and dogmas that keep life locked into inherited injustice and divisive ways. They, like the first century Jerusalem temple, may need to die if the way pioneered by Jesus is to flower afresh. Some welcome change, others resist it. You may be like me, trying to keep a foot in each camp – intellectually acknowledging the death of the old worlds and metaphorical temples that once served us but reluctant to reach toward the sort of change represented by a fuller entry into the way of Jesus.

I think of the human adventure like a journey into an unknown future. Our task is to build a world in which humanity may flourish. We learn to travel together in carriages where we may learn from and with one another. Over time, the carriages get bogged in the soft earth. They stop moving and become castles where we can celebrate our life together and forget the rigours of the journey and the destination we once sought. Eventually, castles (like Downton Abbey perhaps) develop cracks and eventually crumble. The world represented by our castle (or is it our temple?) ends and we are left bewildered and uncertain. Some hardy and spirit-sensitive souls pick themselves up and continue the journey on foot toward peace and justice – they in turn create carriages – that become castles that develop cracks – that crumble – and a few pick themselves up and like Abraham of old continue on the journey.

There's evidence that the economic system we've inherited and shaped to serve first world comfort is like a castle with cracks and might crumble. The term 'safe as a church' is no longer appropriate. The secure world of Christian dogma, ritual, moral standards and predictability are looking suspiciously like a temple ready to fall. The dominance of western attitudes and power is surely coming to an end. Are we living in a time when economic, religious and social 'temples' that have shaped our society are crumbling around the edges- or are they decaying at their heart?

I've gained fresh insight into Mark 13 from a recent commentary by John P. Keenan, an American Anglican who lives with one foot firmly in the Christian church and the other as firmly in the Buddhist tradition. This trans-religious reading of religious texts is one of the exciting frontiers in contemporary biblical and theological study. Commenting on Mark 13 John Keenan recalls that a primary insight of the Buddha is recognition of the impermanence of all things.

Life is not static. It's a process of continuing creation and becoming. Change is written into the very heart of life from world events to personal living and to the sub atomic dimensions of creation. 'There is nothing that remains stable and apart from the constant flow of change.' Every person, every institution, every way of life, every system, every part of creation is provisional and subject to change. Western thinkers have tended to search for stability and the sort of personal security that accompanies sameness.

Mark 13, claims Keenan, presents Jesus undermining stable and static views of life. The temple has fallen. That's what happens in a changing world. Now let's get on with the life of love, peacemaking and justice building. New temple-like structures will emerge and they too will eventually crumble. Returning to the Christian side of his psyche, Keenan observes that it is only when we escape from reliance on the controlling influence of the castles, temples and systems that both shape and cripple life that we're able to sense the ever-fresh presence and call of God who cannot be contained by any human creation. At a personal level, it's not unusual that in times of disorienting grief or loss or sadness beyond description or crippling uncertainty that people sense the presence and energy of God in fresh ways. Mark encourages his readers to keep the faith in spite of the loss of the temple and all it represented. There is a Christ-shaped future to be born even though the form it will take is unclear

In our story, the disciples ask how they might predict the onset of crippling, temple-destroying change. Mark's words, placed in Jesus' mouth, are addressed to the struggling church of the days following the end of the world they had known before the destruction of the temple. Jesus does not deny the pain and disorientation that accompanies the death of those things that have previously given a sense of meaning, stability, security and identity. But the living of the good news he pioneered, the search for a society shaped by the qualities for which Jesus lived must and will continue. Later he'll hint at Jesus' resurrection – a hint that the journey continues led by the living and elusive Christ. This will be the thread that continues rather than the metaphorical and actual temples we create. The continuing thread that holds life together is the spirit of energy and love bequeathed to humanity through Jesus. This alone endures and seeks expression in every age.

Exploring Further

Those who want to explore the work of Keenan and his use of Buddhist wisdom in his work as Christian theologian and biblical scholar will be helped by John P Keenan, *The Gospel of Mark, A Mahayana Reading*, 1995 and *The Wisdom of James, Parallels with Mahayana Buddhism*, 2005. A classic presentation of the Christian way with the help of Buddhist wisdom and practice is Paul Knitter, *Without Buddha I could not be Christian*, 2009. This book, already a classic, is both an introduction to Buddhism and a very helpful rethinking of Christianity.

A writer who gave attention to the relation between openness to change and preservation of what is, was Henry Nelson Wieman (1884-1975). He made a distinction between created good and creative good. 'Created good' is represented by buildings, churches, creeds, political and economic systems and programmes designed to serve human living. They come and go, they are changeable and should not be held on to beyond their ability to serve human flourishing. They should not be worshipped as though they are god - given and unchanging. 'Creative good' is God-spirit flowing through life, drawing people and nations together into new configurations, new expressions of human, new ways of serving human need. Creative good gives birth to created goods but flows on beyond their used by dates. He associates faith with adventurous human commitment to creative good rather than defence of created good.

4

What happened to the good news?
Mark 1:14-20

> We claim to be bearers of good news – but what if our words and living have become bad news for those who most need acceptance, encouragement and energy for life?

The question I would like you to ponder is: what happened to the good news? In today's reading, Mark describes the beginnings of Jesus' ministry among the people of Galilee, a people he knew and valued. To a people struggling to make ends meet and to keep their heads high in a society shaped by the presence of a foreign army of occupation, he claimed to be the bearer of liberating good news. To a people locked into cramped forms of believing and living he brought good news of the extravagant and transforming love of God.

'Gospel' or good news was a common term in the Roman Empire where it was associated with Roman propaganda. News of a military victory by Roman troops, the birth of a royal child, and the accession to power of a new Emperor were all described as glad tidings or 'gospel'. Imperial good news strengthened

Roman power. The good news Jesus taught and lived was to strengthen ordinary people, to lift their sights, build their confidence and empower them for living in a world overflowing with God-presence.

According to Mark's telling of the Jesus story, the first thing Jesus did when he commenced his ministry was to invite a group of people to share his ministry. It's an important declaration that his ministry will not be a solo effort. He'll explore the meaning of good news in the company of others. He needed companions with whom he could explore possibilities and who might mutually encourage one other as they explored what could only be called a revolution in human understanding and living. It's of more than passing interest that Jesus should have chosen workers rather than managers, lay people rather than professors or priests to be his closest friends and colleagues on what would prove to be a costly pilgrimage.

At first reading, the story of these men leaving family and work responsibilities behind while they head off on their journey into life raises a host of questions: What happened to their families in the absence of the primary earner? What about their children who would be deprived of a father's care? What sort of religion requires its most fervent followers to head off to do their thing while others carry the can? Are these disciples following a tradition known in other Eastern faiths whereby a middle years man whose family was off his hands might leave home and head off to discover his inner soul? They're legitimate questions and suggestions but they lie beyond the scope of the key point Mark is seeking to convey to his readers. Mark's a good storyteller but he's an even better theologian. The story of the call of the fishermen is an illustration of what is meant by 'the good news of God' which – according to verse 14 – lay at the heart of what Jesus wanted to share with the people of Galilee.

In a small commentary written by Robert Tannehill, I came across this passage: 'There is nothing to indicate that the previous

What happened to the good news? Mark 1:14-20

life of the disciples was especially evil. But even a life that is not especially evil can be small and cramped. All of us suffer to some extent from cramped lives. Being human, we are small in comparison to the vastness of the universe and the wonder of God. That will not change. But when we become comfortable in our smallness, when our vision becomes limited to our own small desires and purposes, we lose perspective. A blade of grass becomes large for us because we no longer see the towering trees.... The call to discipleship is accompanied by the discovery of a larger world to live in, a purpose greater than our own, a greatness that makes ordinary goods unimportant',

Tannehill's words state something I was feeling for but was unable to name. In calling these disciples Jesus was inviting them to leave the little world they knew and by which they were shaped and to join with him in an exploration of a larger and more generous world than they had dared to imagine. Life as a fisherman, bounded by regulations and work conditions imposed by Roman overlords and in a time-bound village, becomes in our story a symbol for cramped existence. That may sound like a harsh call but remember Mark is making a single point in this parable-like story from the ministry of Jesus. Henceforth, the lives of these four fishermen would be identified with the work of Jesus and to sharing with him in exploring what it means to live in the larger world that is God's good creation. They would explore what it means to escape from the little and cramped perspectives that can easily squeeze life out of existence and instead to live more consistently within the forgiving, liberating and hospitable love of God.

This continues to be the heart of the call to discipleship. The region of Galilee remained the home of our fishermen but they'd been captured by a new way of life – we might say they'd stumbled across a new way of doing life. Recall that in the story of Jesus' baptism by John we're told the heavens were ripped open allowing the love of God to flow freely into every part of life. The disciples, led by Jesus, were to explore what it means to live well in such a world.

The remainder of the Gospel of Mark tells of how Jesus demonstrated what it means to live in the larger world of God's extravagant love. He heals the sick, gathers the ignored and the cast-aside, breaks down barriers that divide, feeds the hungry, forgives the erring and teaches all who will hear that they are of significance within the love of God whatever the status assigned to them by an unjust social and economic system. So Jesus became recognised as an embodiment of the good news of God.

The task of the Christian church is to continue on this journey pioneered by Jesus. The church's mission is to share through words and deeds that life is a gift, that we live in a large world, that God is present within this world and that we, weak as we may be, can share in the ongoing creative work of God. It would be good if the story ended here – knowing that the church took up the task and across the centuries has consistently breathed love, forgiveness, acceptance, generosity and universal hospitality into human communities. Sadly, the expansive good news of God has more often been squeezed into the cramped spaces of a safety-first church wanting cramped obedience rather than inviting to expansive and generous adventure. Sometimes, the good news has been codified into well-rehearsed formulae that, if accepted, become a passport into imagined heavenly bliss following death. The story of how the expansive good news of God's extravagant love has over and over been crammed back into containers dominated by human fear, prejudice and the search for power is the shadow side of the Christian story.

The question before us now is well summed up in an essay by eminent theologian John Cobb, entitled, 'Can Christ become good news again?' Cobb acknowledges the tragedy that has befallen the church as it has sought to confine the expansive message of God in Christ into manageable but cramped creeds, dogmas and, worst of all, prejudices masquerading as morality. He

What happened to the good news? Mark 1:14-20

notes how the good news of Christ soon became bad news for the Jews who across the centuries were treated as scum by the Christian community and were harried, killed and abused in the name of Christ. Christ has not always been good news for those whose lands and religions were colonised or invaded by armies masquerading as bearers of the Christ presence. Christ has not always been good news for women who until recently were denied basic human rights in most Christian communities. Christ has not been good news to many homosexual persons. An earnest and monotonous quoting of a few verses of Scripture has been used as a smoke screen behind which old-fashioned prejudice continues to operate.

Reflecting on these and other examples Cobb asks: 'If Christ is bad news to all these groups, can Christ still be good news to others? The answer is no! For Christ to be good news to any Christ must be good news to all. Universality is an indispensable element in the good news bound up with Christ... If Christ is not good news to all, Christ ceases to be good news for us as well. The question now is, "Can Christ become good news again?" The future of Christianity hangs in the balance.' Cobb again: 'We need a liberating Christ; but Christ cannot liberate unless Christ is liberated from the baggage that has made Christ, for so many, the oppressor'. When Jesus began his ministry in Galilee he proclaimed the good news of God's love and in so doing invited people to leave the cramped thinking and living they had lapsed into and instead to discover a larger world and then to accept their role in weaving universal love and respect into the communities of that world.

Well, can Christ become good news again? Can the church re-enter today's gospel reading? Can the Christian church in all its diversity be converted to its proper self? Are we good news for the lost, the marginalised, the broken and forgotten? How are we doing learning to live in the expanded world into which Jesus invited and still invites his disciples? What about the cramped places in our lives? Inasmuch as we are captured by a vision of divine love at the heart of an expanding world and we're committed to valuing and honouring every person, we have a gift to offer. It's a gift needing to be reclaimed and re-explored every day. Can Christ become good news again?

Exploring Further

In the introduction to the book, *Can Christ become Good News again?* 1991, John B. Cobb begins: 'As a North American Protestant churchman, my greatest hope for the church is for the renewal here of a passionate, progressive Christian faith', and continues, 'nothing is more disheartening than the widespread assumption that only institutionalist, doctrinaire, emotionalist, and legalistic forms of Christianity can evoke passion, that progressive thought waters down Christian conviction and commitment. For one like myself, who sees institutionalist, doctrinaire, emotionalist, and legalistic as distortions of Biblical faith, and who believes that to be faithful is to be free and open, the present situation of the church is cause for acute pain'. Forty years later, Cobb continues to explore the frontiers of living and believing. Google his name and find videos of him speaking of his environmental and economic concerns, his theological insights and his deep concern for our wounded world.

5

Remembering St Francis while Assembly meets

> Church synods, conferences, assemblies and other decision-making groups tend to portray the church at its best and at its miserable worst. Perhaps Saint Francis has important lessons to teach us, or at least to tease us into new imaginings. One year, the Feast of Saint Francis was celebrated on the day a denominational assembly met.

Today, we join with congregations around the world in recalling the life and witness of Saint Francis of Assisi. It may be appropriate we do this on the weekend when the annual church Assembly is meeting. A conversation between the saint and the assembly of the saints might be worth pondering.

Francis was born in 1182 into a wealthy Italian family. He died in 1226. He followed parental and societal expectations and entered upon a military career. At age 20, he was imprisoned, following a skirmish between citizens of Perugia and his native Assisi. In the years that followed, he felt himself to be pursued by God. His response was dramatic. Feeling called to live in continuity with the simple way of life of Jesus he gave up his right to family wealth, set aside military aspirations, embraced poverty as a way of life and held and kissed a leper to signify his intention to identify with the marginalised and needy. He became a preacher of God's love and travelled throughout Italy with others who became his brothers and sisters in faith. They sought to walk as nearly as they could in the footsteps of Jesus. It is interesting to speculate why this somewhat eccentric and fanatical Middle Ages preacher has claimed the interest of Christ followers ever since. Is there something in us that yearns for the simplicity of love and faith within which he dwelt?

Early in his ministry, Francis was at prayer before a crucifix in the little church of San Damiano near Assisi. Tradition says that the crucifix above the altar spoke to him: 'Francis, do you not see how my house is falling into ruin? Go and repair it for me!' Believing the invitation referred to the shambolic state of the building in which he was praying, Francis set about rebuilding the little church. Later, he became aware the invitation to repair the church was to be understood in a deeper sense than the repair of a building. His response was to dedicate his life to the rediscovery and rebuilding of the church understood as a community of ordinary people consciously living within the love of God and serving humanity. It was the inner spirit and actions of the church rather than the windows, roof and downpipes that needed repair. A similar invitation to rebuild or heal the church is the implicit theme and essential business of every church Assembly, Conference and Synod.

Francis was not the only one seeking to rebuild the church at that time. Most notable among contemporary church builders was Pope innocent III (Pope 1198–1216), regarded as one of the most notable and powerful of the medieval Popes. He reinforced the maxim that no one could be saved outside of the Roman Church – a view that has cast a long shadow over world history.

He sought to clarify church doctrine and actively suppressed heretics who pushed the boundaries of belief. Innocent sought to dominate every area of society. He built a church organisation dominated by the power of the great feudal lords with the Pope at the top of the feudal pyramid of power. He initiated the 4th and 5th crusades as expressions of his desire that Jews and Muslims should know themselves to be inferior to Christians. Innocent III, like formidable church leaders in every age, sought to rebuild the church on foundations of centralised power, coercion and domination. This road to rebuilding the church continues into our day in Roman and Protestant, Papist and Calvinist forms.

Francis' path to the rebuilding of the church could not have been more different than the path chosen by Innocent III. His way was shaped by the primacy of love rather than coercive power. He sought to rediscover and to embody the simple love-shaped way of Jesus. Francis represented a somewhat freewheeling and person-centred way of being Christian. He sought to rediscover the Galilean vision of an inclusive, peacemaking, reconciling, forgiving and generous way of life. Like Jesus before him, he identified with the poor of his day and had an uncomplicated affection for the natural world and for animals as companions on life's journey. If Innocent III – like his Roman and Protestant successors of later generations – valued predictability, obedience and straight lines dividing the good from the bad and the faithful from the heretics, Francis lived within the ambiguities of human frailty, sought to break down barriers that divide the human family and valued the journey into love over obedience to creeds, confessions, doctrines and ecclesiastical custom.

I don't want to fall into the trap of identifying the Assembly and its majority as followers of the papal methods of Innocent III (though there may be some similar tendencies!) while at the same time regarding the dissidents among them as contemporary followers of the simpler yet risky pathways of Francis of Assisi.

Life is far more complex than that! Most of us swing between the power seeking ways of Innocent III and the essentially freewheeling simplicity and generosity of Francis. The question is which has priority in our living and our ambitions.

We usually regard the word 'church' as a noun, referring to buildings, organisations, corporate structures, guardianship of moral certainty and stewardship of non-negotiable, divinely revealed truths. In the life and ministry of Francis, the word 'church' functions more like a verb, a doing word, something enacted. 'Church' is something that happens when the values of Jesus are enacted in the world of the everyday. When grace and mercy are injected into situations seemingly ruled by violence, aggression, exclusion or revenge, 'church' happens.

When Francis broke with the military pathway expected of a young man and instead sought to become a peacemaker – 'church' happened. When he embraced a leper as a symbol of his identification with the marginalised and ignored – 'church' happened. When he refused to adhere to the norms of a feudal system that determined who had power and who were regarded as being expendable and instead treated everyone as brother or sister – 'church' happened. When he resolved that possessions were to be shared rather than hoarded and turned his back on the accumulation of wealth – 'church' happened. When, in 1219, during the 5th Crusade, he met with Muslim leader Sultan al Kamil in Egypt and they spoke of peace and reconciliation – 'church' happened. When he took time to meet, listen and learn with someone he had been taught to distrust – 'church' happened. When Francis welcomed animals as friends, the beauty of nature as gift of God – 'church' happened. When he resolved to gather others who followed on the same pathway and determined that their way of relating was to be patterned after the Knights of the Round Table rather than a hierarchical vision of the Christian community – 'church' happened.

Church in the Franciscan mode functions more as a verb, a doing and happening word than as a noun, a static and structured object. 'Church' happens when grace triumphs over judgment, when inclusion crowds out exclusion, when reconciliation overcomes revenge, when honesty crowds out conformity. It seems to me that the healing or rebuilding of the church in our time requires a rediscovery of this Franciscan understanding of church – a love-shaped way of living rather than a network of confessions, creeds and regulations. The essence of this way of being church, Francis wrote in his rule for the guidance of the emerging Franciscan community is to 'follow the teaching and the footprints of our Lord Jesus Christ'. Simple, even simplistic, yet profound beyond easy fulfilment.

Some wonder aloud whether the church is worth rebuilding or healing. Understood as a community of judgment, conformity and centralised power, the church may be surplus to human requirements. At another, more Franciscan level, the world continues to need the church, or better, communities of people who keep alive the words, values and deeds of Jesus and who, like Francis, live for reconciliation, peace, forgiveness, community, inclusion, and generosity, who live within the mystery of divine love made known in Jesus. Church structures come and go, they are always provisional and subject to change but the attitudes and perspectives of Jesus lived out with simplicity, humility, graciousness and consistency are the essence of 'church' understood as a verb.

There was a dramatic moment near the beginning of Francis' ministry when in the presence of his father and the local Bishop, Francis stripped naked signifying his desire to live a life that was transparent, honest and no longer relied on power, wealth or position. Perhaps in this dramatic action there's an important clue for the repairing of the church in our day. The healing of the church requires a naked church – a community that's giving up the desire to control the thinking and believing of its members, a community depending more on the energy of love rather than the exercise of coercive power, a community where all voices are welcomed and the way of Jesus is being explored as though for the first time. A naked church would take itself less seriously and the way of Jesus more seriously

---

Exploring Further

Leonardo Boff, *Saint Francis – a model for human liberation*, 1982, describes Francis as a follower of Jesus the liberator. There are many books about Francis and Boff is among the best. For those interested in Francis' notable meeting with Sultan al Kamil see Paul Moses, *The Saint and the Sultan* 2009.

6

The adventures of church table

1 Corinthians 11:17-22

> Early church gatherings took place around a meal table; food was shared, a reading from the teaching and deeds of Jesus was read and discussed and there were prayers for each other and for the world. At the heart of it all was a domestic table. Perhaps we can learn from the adventures of church table.

You can tell a lot about the theology and worship practices of a congregation by attending to the communion table – its design, its placement, and the purposes for which it's used. I think the church table is the most important piece of furniture in a church building and the item that tells us most about the life of a congregation and the tradition to which they belong. If you want to read the meaning of a church, the table is a good place to begin. Observe how it's placed in relation to the pulpit and which of these two items seems to have priority in the layout. Note whether folk describe their table as an altar or as a table and become aware of the differing theologies that lie behind each term. In some churches, worshippers receive the food from the table while kneeling at a rail. In others, they stand in a circle while in others the bread and wine is taken to worshippers sitting in the pews. Behind each practice is a statement about a congregation's understanding of faith and of church. We shape our church table and then the table shapes us. In my experience Church tables have personality – they're like living beings!

The Christian movement began around simple household tables in the homes of early Christ followers. We're told in Acts 2 that early Christians 'broke bread at home and ate their food with glad and generous hearts'. What eventually came to be called Eucharist, Lord's Supper or Holy Communion, a set apart, ritualised meal, was initially part of a meal eaten around a domestic table. From the 4th century, Christians began meeting in larger buildings and the simple table of earlier times morphed into an altar on which it was claimed the death of Christ was re-enacted if the service took place under the guidance of a properly ordained priest. The belief developed that Christ was literally present in the bread and the wine. Altars were typically set against the back wall of the nave and were constructed of costly materials and were elaborately decorated. They were placed at a distance from the people – a holy place reserved for holy people. The household table was forgotten.

Protestant reformers rejected the Roman sacrificial understanding of Eucharist and it's still common in Protestant churches to have the words placed on the front of the church table: 'Do this in remembrance of me' – a significant liturgical statement in itself but also a declaration that 'we're not Romans – for us, the bread and wine stay what they are and if Christ be present, it's in the gathering of the community rather than focused in bread or wafers, wine or grape juice'. However, the tables in many Protestant churches still look suspiciously like altars. Our St Luke's table is somewhat altar-like with its filled-in panels in front and on the sides. The earlier church on this site had a very small table set under the shadow of a very large pulpit – a clear statement about the priority of the preached Word. Many here will remember the time, not long ago, when white cloths were placed along the backs of pews symbolising that an imaginary table extended into the congregation so that, though people remained anchored to their pews, at least in imagination they fed at a single table.

Church tables have a will of their own and in recent years they've been on the move! Our table is among the movers. From a place toward the back of the nave with the elders chairs behind it, it later snuck up into a place between pulpit and lectern and is now in a central place surrounded on three sides by worshippers. Its new place suggests that community and sharing are primary in our understanding of Christian life.

Like seating at a wedding feast, Church tables have a named place for everyone who cares to come. We don't gather around church table because we're particularly virtuous or pious but because we trust that life is lived within the love of God and each of us is valuable. There's always a place with our name on it at the table of God's love. Church tables are by nature welcoming and inclusive. Traditions that exclude some groups or individuals from the church table have lost the plot. They've given in to society-shaping prejudice. Church tables in such settings weep.

There was no special preparation for our involvement in today's service. We came straight from our homes and occupations, carrying with us whatever worries and troubles, failures and achievements are part of who we are on this particular day. We carry them with us to the table. The table represents the generous love of God at which each of us has a named place. It's a table where human equality within and before God is recognised and celebrated.

Many church tables have a sense of humour. At the Funeral Mass for Pope John Paul II in St Peter's Square in 2005, there was a deliciously serendipitous moment. When it came to the passing of the peace, TV cameras focused on visiting princes, presidents, prime ministers and prelates. President Mugabe, significant contributor to human suffering in Zimbabwe, was sitting near to Prince Charles of the House of Windsor. They were trapped within the ritual. Mugabe reached out his hand to Charles and they passed the peace to each other. The next day, the western media were indignant, suggesting that good Prince Charles had been hoodwinked by the devious Robert Mugabe into shaking hands in public.

I, along with the table set up for the Mass, chuckled at what happened. Inadvertently and unexpectedly, Charles and Robert had, in their handshake and mumbled words about the peace of God, become televised parables of the dream of every church table: that one day enemies will become friends, opponents will become colleagues, lambs and lions will lie down together, and swords shall be beaten into ploughshares. No wonder I detected a smile on the face of the St Peter's church table.

Then there's the compelling story of Sara Miles and her transformative meeting with a wilful church table in a San Francisco church. Sara had had a colourful life, rich in experience and, as a journalist, had lived near to the world's pain. One morning, lost in worry, she walked into St Gregory's Episcopal Church during a celebration of the Eucharist. She had no conscious reason for being there and she was ignorant about church life. Church table was waiting for her. She later wrote: 'I was blown away by the Eucharist, the sharing of bread and the words Jesus welcomes everyone to his table and we offer communion to everyone by name'. She stood by the table in tears. She kept returning and wrote 'Jesus had somehow become lodged in me like a crumb of bread'.

The adventures of church table 1 Corinthians 11:17-22

She later wrote, 'I discovered a religion rooted in the most ordinary yet subversive practice; a dinner table where everyone is welcome, where the poor, the despised, the outcasts are honoured'. A year later, the parish vestry agreed with her that the role of church table should be extended. A church food pantry was opened and each Friday afternoon the church welcomed needy people receiving food from the same holy table used for Sunday Eucharist. She insisted that church table be freed from the piety of life in the sanctuary so it could become a distribution point for the feeding of the hungry. The parish to this day regards Friday afternoon as one of the parish worship services – same table, different people; same spirit, different prayers. Bread and wine on Sunday, food parcels on Friday. No wonder church table at St Gregory's has a smile on its face!

Church tables have a hankering to escape beyond church walls. Teilhard de Chardin was a Jesuit priest and palaeontologist whose work was centred in China. He sought a Christian vision embedded in an evolutionary understanding of life. In 1923, he was in the Ordos Desert in Nth China, far away from churches and Eucharistic tables or altars. Shaped by sensitivity to the power of the table, he allowed his imagination to flow in new directions. He imagined the whole of the universe to be an immense table. He wrote: 'I have neither bread, nor wine, nor altar' so 'I, your priest, will make the whole earth my altar and on it will offer you all the labours and suffering of the world'. He imagined himself gathering into his arms all the beauty and pain in the universe and offering it to God. The division between sacred and secular was broken down as he imagined the energy of the risen Christ pulsating through the universe and drawing everything toward cosmic and human unity. His essay 'The Mass of the World' has become a classic, loved by church tables everywhere who yearn to escape from their set apart churches and to flow freely in the wider world. Imagine a table as vast as the universe!

Teilhard's Mass of the World need not remain in the Ordos Desert. We can regard our own society or even city being like a table served by the love of God. We can join with church tables everywhere in asking: 'Are any groups excluded from the table? Is everyone getting enough food and companionship? How can we make room at the table for newcomers, the neglected and the lonely?' They're questions gifted to us by the Ecumenical Society of church tables.

Exploring Further

Sara Miles, *Take this bread*, 2008 is a modern day classic, profound in its simplicity. For those not familiar with the life and wisdom of Teilhard de Chardin, one of the greatest of twentieth century Christian thinkers, Ursula King, *Spirit of Fire, the life and vision of Teilhard de Chardin*1998, is a good place to begin. It will whet your appetite for his writings on religion and science, an evolutionary view of God and of earth valuing spirituality.

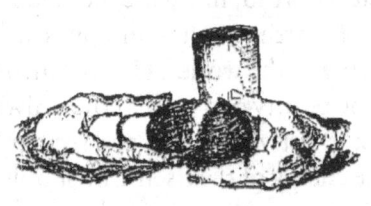

7

Orientation to a new congregation

> How do you become a member of a congregation, how are you introduced to the particular way of being Christian that belongs to this people in this place at this time? How are younger people introduced to the Way? How are long-time members sustained in lively faith? In a wintry time like ours, we may need to be more intentional about the way we attend to such important questions. It is more important to know how to do faith rather than to believe creeds. I wish I'd been more aware of these things fifty years ago. A wee snippet from a sermon – another possibility lost in the walk from pew to meeting room!

I find myself wondering what sort of orientation should be offered to those who seek to become part of our church communities. In his helpful book, *The Buddha and the Christ*, Leo Lefebure, another whose faith has been enriched by participation in Buddhist wisdom and practice, describes his arrival at a Thai Buddhist monastery for what he anticipated would be enlightening conversations about the intricacies of Buddhist and Christian theologies. To his surprise, he was invited to a series of lessons in the practice of meditation. Lefebure wrote: 'I had come to learn about Buddhism, but my first lesson was that Buddhism is not a matter of talking, of discussing doctrines and beliefs, of comparing ideas about human existence and the universe'. He was invited as his initiation to 'do' rather than discuss the Buddhist way.

What sort of initiation might accompany the inclusion of new members into our Christian congregations? Would it include learning and practising the skills of peacemaking? What about learning how we pray in our community? How about seminars on what it means to dwell in the Bible and to live in continuity with the way pioneered by Jesus? Should there be skill sessions on the art of inclusion in an exclusionary and somewhat tribal world? Should there be seminars on the art of forgiveness and the gifting of new beginnings? What about seminars on 'discovering friendship in the presence of difference'? How to lobby local bodies and government about climate change and other important issues? How long would this orientation take (six months, two years? Continuing?) As the world changes, we all need constant re-orientation to the Way. Who would lead our courses? Would the seminars be advertised in the local media? Would there be a general invitation to whoever wants to join in our ongoing exploration of the Way? Can we learn how to 'do' and explore the Jesus Way rather than talk about creeds, rituals, warm hearts and churches? Is this the new face of evangelism, recruitment to the Way of Jesus?

Exploring Further

Leo Lefebure's book *The Buddha and the Christ: Explorations in Buddhist and Christian Dialogue* was published by Orbis Books in 1993.

REDISCOVERING JESUS AND THE WAY HE PIONEERED

While it has become fashionable for people to simply ignore church and what they imagine it represents, I wonder if western society has given up on Jesus too quickly. We need symbols and exemplars of what life can become, of possibilities to be explored, of pathways into a future where every person and their cultural values is appreciated, respected and enabled to contribute to a just and caring society. Jesus represents an evolutionary possibility for humanity. He explored what could be; he pushed his hearers and companions to the edge of possibility and promised that his energy and God-awareness would accompany them on their journey into a reinvented future.

Jesus lived within the purposes of God with such consistency and grace that it's appropriate to describe and to remember him as unique and of universal significance. So, the early church adopted a cluster of titles for Jesus, like 'Son of God', 'Messiah' and 'Son of Man', as their way of describing his significance for their time, their people, and their place. For us in our day to describe Jesus and the possibilities he embodied as representing a crucial and universal 'evolutionary possibility' for humanity is among the ways we might describe his significance for us in our time – our equivalent to the transformative and significant titles given him in the first few centuries of the Christian adventure. The Way pioneered by Jesus is bigger than the life he lived in Palestine – it is a light shining down the corridors of history, summoning us into a future yet to be born and the binding of those who will into a community of Jesus-Spirit.

Renewal of Christian integrity involves an ever-fresh discovery of the life transforming Way pioneered by Jesus. My use of the word 'pioneering' attached to the Way that claimed Jesus is important. Jesus does not represent a set of rules chiselled into concrete slabs, but rather a way of living, a style of life, that needs to be rediscovered, re-explored and re-expressed in every generation, every culture and nation. The resurrection stories symbolise for us that the Way of Jesus continues as contemporary possibility and evocative symbol of what the future can become. Renewal of Christian integrity and contribution to the healing of our world will involve a fresh discovery of the Jesus Way as pioneered in the first century and, crucially, as continuing possibility in every time and place.

There's an important scholarly debate taking place among Biblical scholars as to whether the words assigned to Jesus in the Gospels are an accurate record of what he actually said or whether they are the creation of early church communities, imaginative attempts to convey what they understood to be the meaning and relevance of Jesus and the Way he pioneered. The same question is asked about the deeds of Jesus – did they happen as recorded or are many of them creations of the earliest Gospel writers whose imaginations were shaped by first century understandings of how deep truth is best conveyed. It is a fascinating debate.

I speak of the words and deeds of Jesus without always passing judgment on their historicity. We simply cannot be certain what the historical Jesus actually said (what could have been recorded on a tape recorder) and what he literally did (what could have been recorded with a video). But we do have a pretty good awareness of what he was on about and the sort of things he taught – enough to build a life on. Throughout the centuries, Christian preachers and thinkers have built on the Gospel stories and sayings, expanding their relevance, imagining they were spoken into their time, questioning, inviting and inspiring listeners living far beyond the time in which Jesus lived and spoke. So the words and deeds of Jesus as written in the Gospels become both part of our history and invitation to who we are becoming, sounding boards against which we measure what life can become.

1

Who is this man?

Matthew 21:1-11

> Why read about and explore the thought and life of someone who lived 2,000 years ago? Why place his first-century wisdom alongside twenty-first century discoveries about the immensity and intricacy of our universe and the healing insights of medical experts, psychotherapists and social scientists of our time? The short answer is that Jesus represents a way of living that is needed in our broken and threatening times. The cleverer we become, the more we need the wisdom embodied by Jesus and other life-enhancing pioneers.

Today's Gospel reading tells of the day when the 'Lord of the Dance', the freewheeling Galilean preacher, healer and social reformer, arrived in the national centre of political, religious and economic power – the important city of Jerusalem. Jesus' arrival in the city was a carefully staged piece of street theatre. He'd travelled from the villages of rural Galilee with a pilgrim group who thought of him as among the prophets and were attracted by his message of radical love. Like him, they sought a society that provided a secure place for the poor, the needy and the overlooked. Passover week was, and is, the Jewish time to remember and re-enter dramatic events believed to have taken place long ago when Jewish ancestors, enslaved within an unjust system, under the leadership of Moses escaped from captivity in Egypt. The Galilean pilgrims accompanying Jesus sought escape from contemporary forms of slavery. Perhaps they thought and hoped, 'The revolution might begin this week!'

For three years, Jesus had been pioneering new ways of sensitivity to the presence of God. He'd shared his discoveries with villagers and fisher folk of Galilee and had gathered a community who shared his sensitivity to God and his dream of a just and peaceable society. He'd become known as a healer, a weaver of parables that overturned taken-for-granted wisdom and as a man who welcomed outcasts and the poor to share his life and his food. He acknowledged the traditions of his people but when it came to meeting human need and the development of a more just and hospitable society, he chose love of people over loyalty to inherited rules. He refused to be controlled by barriers that tradition had erected to divide people into the good and the bad, the acceptable and the rejected, family and foreigners. He told the poor, the dispossessed and the marginalised that God, the very energy and foundation of all life, shared their struggles. To the proud, the powerful and the beneficiaries of Roman rule he was a pain in the neck who never stopped questioning values and attitudes they took for granted.

Now he brings his message to the leadership of the nation, hoping for acceptance but fearful of rejection. Like a prodigal son of Israel who has left the security and safety of his home, he had for three years explored the edges of life's possibilities, rediscovering God as enlivening spirit who could not be tamed or held within the legalities of human systems. This wandering son of Israel, returns to the centre of the nation's life to test whether he will be embraced as a brother and invited to share in Passover celebrations or excluded as an erring and misguided rabble rouser.

Tales of his unorthodox ways would have filtered through to the chief priests and rulers in Jerusalem and it comes as no surprise that they, along with others, asked who this man was who entered the holy city through a back gate accompanied by a rabble. It's a simple and uncomplicated question but there has never been a single, unequivocal and universally accepted answer to the question.

A standard text on the historical Jesus written fifty years ago began with a chapter entitled 'Jesus: the man who fits no formula'. It's an insight worth hanging on to. Jesus belongs to every age and every culture yet fits no mould that we might create. There is no fully satisfactory, first-century answer to the question 'who is this man?' Nor is there a twenty-first century answer without loose ends - no answer not open to revision at a later time or in a different place. The Christian church may be a world-wide community united by memory of Jesus and devotion to the way of life he pioneered but we are also divided by our differing responses to the Palm Sunday question, 'who is this man?'

Jesus has become a figure who represents the most daring hopes of humanity as they are expressed anew and differently in each age and in every circumstance. As the hopes vary so do the responses to the question about his identity. Jesus needs to be freshly re-appropriated in each culture, each society and every age, interpreted in words and lifestyles that bring healing in each new setting.

Over the last fifty years or so, there has been a literal explosion of responses to the question 'who is this man?' The answers vary depending on who asks the question and the social, political and spiritual circumstances within which they live. Oppressed people may speak of Jesus the Liberator. Women have sought understandings of Jesus that enhance and value their contribution to life's journey. Some living in Muslim, Hindu or Buddhist societies ask if we can re-interpret Jesus in categories belonging to these great sister faiths. Talk of Jesus the Jew is commonplace. Others seek for distinctively Aboriginal, Maori or 'Queer' responses to the question, 'who is this man?' African theologians speak of 'Christ the Ancestor' while others living in an age dominated by scientific discovery ask how we might speak of Jesus in an evolutionary and interconnected universe. Hitler tragically encouraged the articulation of a race-based Aryan understanding of Jesus. Understandings of Jesus that support white male supremacy are still present.

In a fascinating 2003 book, *American Jesus*, Stephen Prothero describes how successive generations of North American Christians have created interpretations of Jesus that are little more than projections of their personal anxieties or patriotic aspirations. He's been portrayed as 'Sweet Saviour', 'Capitalist Businessman', 'Superstar', 'Super Patriot and leader of the Redeemer Nation', 'Manly Redeemer and founder of Muscular Christianity'. Prothero includes an illustration of Jesus the boxer, his muscles rippling as he prepares to do battle with foreign evil. There seems to be no end to how the Palm Sunday question can be answered.

What of us? Who is this man whose death and ongoing presence we celebrate at Easter time? Some of the ways Jesus has been and is understood are clearly just plain cranky and are far removed from any honest and informed grappling with the words and deeds of Jesus as recorded in the Gospels. The most helpful interpretations emerge from a thoughtful willingness to be deeply questioned by the words and deeds of the Gospel Jesus. The more important thing about the Gospels is not just what they meant when first written but how they question us who read and ponder them in a later generation, surrounded by problems that could not possibly be foreseen in the first century. The essence of Christian living is not that we live in a neat package called 'orthodoxy' that we protect at all costs but that we are willing to be questioned by the church's memory of this man who calls us to live more deeply within love, to seek after peace, to treat all people with respect, to contribute to the healing rather than the destruction of human community. The question 'who is he' spills over into the companion question, 'who am I and who can I become?'

Among the things that led some to oppose Jesus during the final week in Jerusalem was his apparently cavalier attitude toward the letter of the law. They despised him as a 'Liberal' whose attitudes – if taken seriously – would lead to changes that might disrupt current power structures. The word Liberal may be like a red rag to a bull in some circles but it's a perfectly adequate word to describe the Gospel Jesus. One of the greatest of twentieth-century New Testament scholars, Ernst Kasemann, in words that were controversial at the time described Jesus: 'Jesus was a liberal because in the name of God and in the power of the Holy Spirit he interpreted and appraised Moses, the scriptures and dogmatics from the point of view of love and thereby allowed devout people to remain human and even reasonable'. (Is he implying that some 'devout people' may be inhuman and unreasonable?)

Kasemann described how Jesus was devout in his love for God and liberal in his refusal to be bound by traditions that damage one's neighbour. We might understand ourselves as Liberals in this sense, allowing ourselves to be questioned by Jesus' words and deeds while refusing to be imprisoned by any way of being Christian, any dogma or doctrine that damages other people. The rulers and high priests in first-century Jerusalem were too busy defending their own comfort to allow themselves and their systems of privilege to be questioned by the Lord of the Dance and his invitation to newness.

Exploring Further

Jaroslav Pelikan's *The Illustrated Jesus through the Centuries, his place in the history of culture*, 1997, is a beautiful book for those wanting to reflect on how Jesus has been spoken of and followed over the centuries. Gregory Barker (ed.), *Jesus in the World's Faiths – leading thinkers from five religions reflect on his meaning*, 2005, will take you beyond the boundaries of churchly thinking.

2

Cradles into which Jesus was born

Matthew 2:1-12

> My first hearing of a bit of the Jesus story was when as a very small boy, my grandmother took me to a Christmas service at a small Congregationalist church that has long since been dismantled. Back home, she told me the story and I was mesmerised by the tale of shepherds and wise men, angels and mother, a manger and the inevitable sheep, goats and cows that witnessed this special birth. I'm still pondering these ancient parable-like stories.

As I thought about the gospel lesson for today, I kept being drawn back to the first verse telling us that Jesus was born 'in the time of King Herod'. I moved from there to think of the various cradles into which Jesus was born, according to Matthew's birth story

The first cradle that held Jesus was his mother's arms. In Christmas services around the world, this will have been the centrepiece of pageants presented by the children – the Christ child cradled in his young mother's arms. The same theme is present in many of the hymns sung in preparation for Christmas. Jesus is cradled in his mother's arms as though to confirm the more recent recognition that mothers are a child's first god-figure – a presence that nurtures, guides, supports, feeds and is always there. There's something compelling about the birth of a vulnerable child embedded in a community's affirmation that in this child is found the deepest truth about life's meaning and promise.

We may identify with words of philosopher Alfred North Whitehead as he reflected on the birth and subsequent life of Jesus: 'The essence of Christianity is the appeal to the life of Christ as a revelation of the nature of God and of his agency in the world... there can be no doubt as to what elements in the record have evoked a response from all that is best in human nature. The mother, the Child, and the bare manger; the lowly man, homeless and self-forgetful, with his message of peace, love, and sympathy: the suffering, the agony, the tender words as life ebbed, the final despair; and the whole with the authority of supreme victory'. The image of God fully present in a vulnerable child and later a misunderstood adult has contributed to the central Christian affirmation that God is present in weakness: vulnerable love bearing the cost of human reconciliation and becoming.

The child cradled in his mother's arms has become a primary image and embodiment of Christian faith. It stands in stark contrast to images that suggest God to be a powerful and judgmental dictator. In the second part of today's gospel reading, the vulnerability of the child is intensified with the story of his family fleeing from the murderous ways of Herod and becoming refugees. The man of whom it was later said that he had nowhere to lay his head began life as a refugee, rejected by the country of his birth, part of a pilgrim family in search of safety and a place to live. Here perhaps is a clue as to where we might find the footsteps of Christ in our day. Those who follow the way of the Christ child claim no status for themselves. They are servants of humanity, sharing the same vulnerability and operating with no power but the power of love.

The first verse of our reading draws attention to a less hospitable, less comfortable cradle into which Jesus was born. He was born 'in the time of King Herod'. He was cradled by the fears, disappointments and pain engendered by the rule of this man. Those who first valued and meditated on the Gospel of Matthew lived in challenging times and were sensitive to the tough edges of life. The phrase 'the time of King Herod' would have carried meaning for them. 'Herod' was embedded in their cultural memory as a tyrant who had done enormous damage to their recent ancestors.

Emperor Caesar Augustus had appointed Herod 'King of the Jews' and he ruled for about 40 years (37BCE – 4CE). Though a Jew by birth, he was utterly loyal to the Empire and to the way of life it represented. His primary task was to maintain Roman Imperial control in the eastern Mediterranean, ruling over what was like a buffer state intended to hold the line against powerful empires of the East. Herod was devoted to raising the maximum financial return for Rome through the collection of taxes and land tithes.

His name became a by-word for cruelty. When in 37BCE he besieged Jerusalem wholesale massacre ensued and masses of people were butchered. He had little regard for the cultural and religious values of the Jewish people. He rebuilt the Temple in Jerusalem but placed a Roman eagle above the entrance gate as a not too subtle reminder of who was really in charge. He engaged in extensive building projects and filled the country with temples and other buildings – all dedicated to Caesar. It seems he went out of his way to offend the sacred traditions of Palestinian people. He claimed to be King by the will of God and strangely believed he had brought peace and prosperity to the tiny nation.

Cradles into which Jesus was born Matthew 2:1-12

A 'police state' atmosphere pervaded Palestine. Josephus, in his history of the period wrote: 'No meeting of people was permitted nor was walking together or being together permitted – those caught were put to death... as for the rest of the populace, he demanded they submit to taking a loyalty oath that they would maintain a friendly attitude to his rule. Most yielded to this demand out of fear but those who objected he got rid of. When a group of scholars and their students conspired to cut down the great eagle erected over the temple they were burned alive'. So Jesus was born into the pain of a suffering people. He was cradled in the dreams of a people reaching toward a time when the ancient dreams of their people for a time of peace and justice might be realised.

Jesus was born in 4BCE, the final year of Herod's long reign. As the old tyrant aged, repression intensified. Villages around Nazareth were decimated and destroyed about this time – males were murdered, females raped and children enslaved. It is certain that as Jesus grew up he would have learned of this major event in the recent story of Nazareth – 'the day the Romans came'. He would have heard stories and felt the pain of neighbours and family whose lives were changed forever by the coming of the Roman military to their area. He might have wondered, as did others: 'Where was God that day the Romans came?' There's no evidence that Herod had all the children killed as reported in verse 16 of our reading but it was a believable story to those whose families had suffered at the tyrant's hands.

In placing Jesus' birth in Bethlehem, Matthew affirms Jesus was also cradled in the hopes and stories of his ancestors. Bethlehem – according to the scholars – was the place where a saviour would be born, who would lead this people into freedom and peace. In his Gospel, Matthew portrays Jesus as the 'New Moses' who, like the great Moses, will liberate his people, leading them out of the darkness of oppression, binding them into a new community and through their efforts creating a new society built on strong foundations of peace, justice and hospitality. Moses was born into the times of an oppressive Pharaoh just as Jesus was born into the time of Herod.

As Jesus grew, he would have felt the story of Moses becoming his story. Matthew suggests that just as Moses gave the people the 10 commandments, Jesus shared the Sermon on the Mount. He divided important teaching of Jesus into five major addresses suggesting a parallel with the five books attributed to Moses. Jesus was to live out of the history of his people and into the future they dreamed of. He was literally cradled in the dreams and stories of his people. We are foolish to neglect our history and the wisdom it bequeaths to us.

The fourth cradle into which Jesus was born according to today's Gospel was the cradle of accumulated and emergent human wisdom. The visit of the wise men from the east is an acted-out affirmation that Jesus is born within universal human wisdom, the human search for what is good and true and serves human flourishing. We cannot be absolutely certain what group Matthew intended the wise men from the east to represent. Certainly the East was regarded as a place of suspicion and the home of traditional enemies – Babylonians, Assyrians, Persians and Parthians. It is likely, however, the men from the East are Zoroastrian priests. The likely home of the great religions that endure to this day was in the area now known as Uzbekistan, north of present day Iran and Afghanistan.

Perhaps 3,000 years before the time of Jesus, a form of religious wisdom developed on the Eurasian steppes that carried many of the great life themes that were to be developed by later great religions. Their views, aided by the domestication of the horse, spread through the known world – south into the Persian plateau, giving birth to Zoroastrian Faith – east into India where all the great variety of understandings we now describe as Hinduism would flourish – west into the Mediterranean basin, influencing Jewish and Greek religions. It provided the glue that held the great Persian Empire together.

There is no scholarly certainty about the origins or development of Zoroastrianism but it is agreed that religious views found in other enduring religions found their original impulse within this ancient religious pathway. They were among the first to explore the oneness of God. They regarded human history as a struggle between good and evil, light and darkness and they awaited the coming of a saviour or Shayoshan who would bring in a new era. Tracing the 'Z factor' in Jewish, Christian and Muslim Holy Books has become an exciting frontier in religious study – watching out for echoes of direct or indirect Zoroastrian influence.

Jesus, according to Matthew, was born into the cradle of universal human wisdom represented by Zoroastrian visitors, wise men from the distrusted East. Sadly the later church took Jesus from this universal cradle and set him against all other expressions of human wisdom. So those of other faiths became enemies to be overcome rather than colleagues in the search for humane society. The Bible came to be read through eyes shaped by hostility rather than hospitality. In our day, the church, or some parts of it, are learning how to live from hospitality rather than hostility toward those who believe differently or are stewards of other expressions of accumulated and needed human wisdom. Jesus is still best understood within the circle of accumulated human wisdom.

Today, the church, an ambiguous, fault-ridden, fragile, vulnerable human community, cradles Jesus. And how's that going? Well, that's worth exploring.

Exploring Further

The western world has lost Christmas as a celebration of the birth of someone who represents the possibility of justice, peace, God-presence, hospitality and newness. At its best, it's a pleasant occasion for a family gathering and shared frivolity. At its worst, it has become merely an intensification of retail spending, fuelled by deceptive advertising. For the gathered church, it represents a cluster of stories that may not be historical in a literal sense but explored within their original social setting represent possibilities for human existence and help define the Way of Jesus.

For those wanting to set the ancient nativity tales into their original socio-political setting and to sense the liberating message originally heard by an oppressed people, Richard Horsley, *The Liberation of Christmas – The infancy narratives in social context*, 1989, is very helpful. A brief introduction to Zoroaster is available in Richard C. Foltz, *Spirituality in the Land of the Noble – how Iran shaped the world's religions*. 2004. The Zoroastrian community is not large today but its presence is a reminder of historic links between religions that later became competitors.

3

Living in the wilderness in the spirit of Jesus
Matthew 4:1-11

> There's little doubt we live in two possible worlds – the popular world of get more, gain power, be popular; and a world of service, simplicity and hospitality as pioneered by Jesus. Being conscious of the conflict is part of life, learning how to choose, compromise, negotiate our way between two ways is something we're involved in on a daily basis.

Matthew's Gospel tells the story of Jesus' life as the journey of a spiritually and socially sensitive man on a pilgrimage into deepening love. He is depicted as a pioneer of new ways of human living. As though to prepare his readers for conflicts that will follow Jesus throughout his ministry, Matthew begins his narrative with an imaginative tale of Jesus being tested in the wilderness – caught between the call of his deepest dreams and expectations projected by the society in which he lived. Words of a recent hymn (*Great God, your love has called us here* by Brian Wren) describe our human plight – 'half free, half bound by inner chains, by social forces swept along; by powers and systems close confined yet seeking hope for humankind'. The words describe well the experience of Jesus in the wilderness, the struggles of the Christian community in Antioch for which Matthew crafted his re-telling of the Jesus story and the situation in which sensitive twenty-first century Christians find themselves – captured and shaped by powers and systems that deny the priority of servant love as the indispensable glue that holds life together and serves human renewal.

There are many interesting facets of the Temptations story that cry out to be explored but I will limit myself to a brief comment on each of three key words or ideas. Reference to the Wilderness describes a place of aloneness, of uncertainty and struggle. It conjures up memories of Moses leading a people through a desert wilderness wondering how they might become a community shaped by justice, compassion and peace. In the Bible 'the wilderness' is a place of uncertainty and weakness but it's also celebrated as a place where God-awareness may grow and new futures be glimpsed.

The Christian community in Antioch would have readily identified with Jesus in the wilderness. They were a small community, divided by culture and race, trying to remain loyal to the tradition of Moses while also following the distinctive way of Jesus. It was not simple being a Jesus follower in Antioch in the final decades of the first century. Some likened it to being in a small boat on a tempestuous sea and wondering if the fragile ship of faith would survive the storm (Matthew 8:23-27).

Mention of Satan has troubled people over the centuries. It's enough to say that awareness of demonic or satanic influence in life does not commit one to believing in little fork-tailed creatures tempting people to be naughty as depicted by medieval artists. Talk of the Demonic or of Satan is a first-century way of referring to an inner negative spirituality embedded in economic, political, religious and social systems, that draws people away from the peace-loving, generous and justice-seeking purposes of

God embodied and taught by Jesus and the prophets, forces that distort human living and deny the possibility of life together in compassion-shaped community distort human living and deny the possibility of life formed by community.

The title 'Son of God' used by the tempter in our story is an important clue as to Matthew's understanding of the nature of the demonic in his time. The original readers of Matthew's Gospel knew there was already a man described as 'Son of God' – it was among the titles given to the Roman Emperor whose will was to be obeyed at all times and whose power was supreme and incontestable. The words addressed to Jesus, 'if you are the Son of God' take us to the heart of the conflict between followers of the Jesus way and custodians of the Roman Empire. To suggest Jesus was 'Son of God' was to claim the way of life he pioneered, embodied and taught was an alternative and more life-enhancing way of life than that represented by the Roman Emperor. Jesus, the preacher of love-shaped peace, generosity and forgiveness, it is suggested, is the true 'Son of God' and not the all-powerful Emperor imposing his form of 'peace' by brutal force and fear. It was a counter-cultural and revolutionary claim.

Roman rule in Palestine is the ever-present background to all parts of the New Testament. There was no escaping its presence – reminders of Roman power and authority were everywhere – in buildings devoted to the Emperor, Jewish religious rituals reshaped to serve Imperial purposes, a cruel military presence, a growing gap between the wealthy 10% and the 90% near or beneath the bread line, systemic injustice justified by imperial greed, the poor marginalised and strangers distrusted. Jesus was remembered as the leader of a social and spiritual renewal movement that built an alternative way to that represented by the all-pervasive Roman influence that was as pervasive in first century Palestine as was apartheid in South Africa or Nazism in Germany in the twentieth century. The New Testament Gospels are handbooks for folk who have chosen the path of Jesus rather than obedience to Roman power.

The story of the Temptations of Jesus depicts Jesus choosing to resist rather that cooperate with the demands of the all-pervasive influence of the Empire. He actively rejects a life shaped by a search for power, prestige, popularity and possessions. This rejection of the Imperial template for human living led to increasing conflict with those who benefited from the Roman presence and eventually to his death. Our gospel reading is a summary of his whole life – lived in the wilderness but within an alternative dream of what might be. His responses to demonic temptation remind me of conversations I had with brave South African church members when I visited their troubled nation in the apartheid years. In a wilderness time they were choosing to live within the counter-cultural way of Jesus. The story of Jesus in the wilderness had become their story.

The Roman Empire no longer exists but powerful and all-pervading systems that drive the world in directions diametrically opposed to the life-enhancing way of Jesus are alive and well. The demonic is embedded in powers and systems that, though promising all sorts of goodies, in fact serve destructive ends. American theologians frequently speak of the American Empire, subtle, aggressive and determined to spread its influence and acting in ways that parallel those of the Roman Empire. The human community in the twenty-first century is held in the all-pervading embrace of an economic system, Global Free-Market Capitalism, that promotes greed rather than compassion as a desirable and primary virtue, that justifies the destruction of the environment in the pursuit of unshared wealth, that divides human communities between the haves and the never haves, that leads to wars fought over access to raw materials to feed market-God and made possible by an out of control and unregulated armaments industry – and much more.

Our global free-market economic system functions like an all-knowing, all-powerful God, shaping human consciousness and punishing those who sin against its commands. The failure of existing economic structures to serve human flourishing is increasingly being recognised by sensitive people, including Pope Francis, theologians in all faiths and even some commercial leaders who though directly benefitting from lopsided and unjust systems are asking if we need to listen afresh to inherited religious wisdom, including that of Jesus.

But the pathway to human and environmental renewal will be long and costly. It is difficult to pursue the Jesus-shaped vision of life, formed by peace, sharing, compassion and generosity within the all-pervasive amoral environment represented by our dominant economic system. Its subtle values and attitudes are everywhere – around us and in us. It has become an all-pervasive religion. Like first century Palestinians, like Jesus, like sensitive Christians across the centuries, we live in a wilderness time. Quite simply, it is difficult to live the Jesus way in a culture promoting greed, exploitation, division and violence. Is the story of Jesus in the wilderness our story?

I imagine Mathew sitting down on the first day of the week and discussing with new Christians in Antioch what it means to live in wilderness times. He would have read the story of the temptations and then hurried on to what follows in his version of the Jesus story. Immediately after the Temptations story, he describes Jesus inviting people to become part of a community of the alternative way, a people learning together how they might follow the Jesus way in wilderness times. He would have discussed the Sermon on the Mount, a sort of spiritual and moral direction-finder for a people living in wilderness times. As was their custom each Sunday, the Christian community in Antioch would have shared bread and wine, the food of the poor, prayed for the coming of the God-Kingdom in the words of the Jesus Prayer and almost certainly recited, chanted or sang what we have come to call the

Beatitudes. In a wilderness time, they were exploring how they might live for a more humane future than that represented by the Empire.

I don't know what the future form of the church will be – what I do know is that humanity needs groups of people who recall, share and live within the words and deeds of Jesus – people who live in the wilderness in the spirit of Jesus, trusting that within the love of God, their efforts, their prayers, their struggle contribute to the healing of the world.

Exploring Further

> I find myself returning over and over to the sentiments in the last paragraph. There's no doubt we live in wilderness times. The church is ailing, in many cases uncertain as to whether its congregations can even survive let alone contribute meaningfully to the healing of our broken world, speak a word of hope, recruit disciples from a younger age group, rethink belief in a new age. Commentaries help us understand what the Biblical story might have meant in Biblical times but it is up to us as members of today's wounded church to interpret what it means to live in our wilderness time. It's a time for bold imagining and risky action. Who must take the initiative in reaching toward new ways of being church? Or do we just give up? Big decisions.

4

Jesus' homecoming sermon
Luke 4:16-30

> In some Protestant traditions, it's a custom that a Minister seeking to move to a new parish is asked to preach in that parish before a decision is made whether the receiving congregation agree that she/he is the one for them. Jesus failed the test so became an itinerant preacher and spiritual guide.

For Luke, this story of Jesus' homecoming to the synagogue at Nazareth, along with the response of those who thought they knew him well, is crucial for understanding all that follows in Luke's retelling of the Jesus story. This passage, like Paul's hymn to love (1 Corinthians 13) that was also read today, is a declaration that in Jesus a new mode of human existence is offered to humanity. Each of these passages presents a critique of much that we take for granted in human living along with a summons to new ways of living within the human family and within God – love.

Jesus, it seems, was becoming known and was praised for his activity and teaching throughout Galilee. Now he returned to those who had watched him grow up to explain what he was up to and to share the deep convictions that were shaping his activity.

But something went wrong at Nazareth. A day that began well turned ugly as those who at first welcomed him to their synagogue and even invited him to preach were gripped by an irrational fury that could have led to his death. What went wrong? Why such a powerful and negative response to Jesus' words? Within the story are important clues to understanding the nature of Jesus' ministry and the style of living he pioneered in Palestine but bequeathed to humanity.

It would have surprised many when Jesus chose to read from Isaiah 61: 'The Spirit of the Lord is upon me because he has anointed me to bring good news to the poor. He has sent me to proclaim release to the captives and recovery of sight to the blind, to let the oppressed go free, to proclaim the year of the Lord's favour'. They were well-known words that represented hopes few thought could ever be achieved. For Jesus, however, these words encapsulated the motivation and spiritual impetus that lay behind his work as a servant of God's purposes. According to Luke, they represent a sort of manifesto or mission statement – words Jesus intended to embody and bring to life in a society where too many people were denied a fair go in life. Synagogue discussion that day took on a new urgency when Jesus declared that in the renewal movement he was initiating, these well-known words were being taken out of the cupboard where imaginative but seemingly impossible dreams are stored and were being fulfilled in the real world.

'The year of the Lord's favour' was commonly regarded as a reference to the year of Jubilee described in Leviticus 25. As part of the rebuilding of the Israelite nation following the tough years of exile, and aware that over time injustices creep into the fabric of any society, visionary leaders of that time proposed that every fifty years there should be an economic and social audit of the nation's life. Debts were to be cancelled, land returned to its original owners, slaves were to be freed and the land was to lie fallow. It was to be a year ruled by generosity, justice and hospitality for all, including slaves and animals.

There's no evidence that the nation ever fully enacted this somewhat utopian legislation but it kept its place within the nation's holy book as a reminder that People of God should never regard injustice or poverty as inevitable. Humans create injustice and humans can eliminate it, if they have the will to do so. It must have been a dramatic moment when Jesus declared that his ministry was an announcement and enactment of a Jubilee year. He would live and teach the Jubilee way and invite others to share with him in the renewal of their society. His life task will be to release people from failure, point towards the renewal of social and economic life and to befriend those currently on the margins of life. As Jubilee Man, he will be an agent of new beginnings for individuals and for the communities to which they belong.

The first impulse of Jesus' hearers, perhaps not fully grasping the revolutionary implications of what he was saying, was to welcome this daring announcement. Initial enthusiasm, however, was soon replaced by scepticism that someone from a Nazareth family they all knew could lead such a dramatic and adventurous renewal movement when others had failed. Then the day and the mood turned ugly. Jesus hit a raw spot when he recalled stories of how in the time of the prophets Elijah and Elisha, God acted in a healing manner among foreigners, known enemies of Israel's ambitions. The implication is that the Jubilee is for all people, not just for Israelites. God apparently acts on a larger canvas than the one they know. This, they regard as unacceptable – the suggestion that others are included in God's love and that God is present in healing ways in cultures, nations and religions other than their own must be rejected lest their own 'specialness' in the eyes of God be compromised.

Why the murderous anger? Surely it's good news that God's love has no boundaries and that signs of Divine presence are to be found within every nation and culture. But the people of

Nazareth – like many before and since – had an interest in denying full humanity and respect to those they regarded as enemies. They needed enemies, outsiders, and scapegoats. It's a human phenomenon that continues into our day. We seem to need some one or group, culture or nation on whom we can project blame for defects and difficulties in life. The identification of so-called 'enemies' helps create a sense of unity in a society and mobilises energy though usually in destructive directions. It's even claimed by politicians and religious leaders that it's God's will that we condemn, fight, and destroy those who, by tradition or political convenience, are described as 'enemy'. We can observe it in the larger world of politics but it's also present in the smaller world of everyday living.

A few years ago, I found myself caught up in a silly dispute when, in preaching at an Auckland church, I suggested that the spirit of God was present in religions other than Christianity and that we could learn from their deep wisdom while also sharing with them our deep wisdom we have gained from Jesus and the Way he pioneered. I suggested that God painted on a larger canvas than the one we had inherited. This I presented as 'good news' but complaints were made, meetings held, a petition floated, a complaint laid and feathers ruffled. Remarkable! The irony in all this was that the resident Minister claimed to believe the same things but was smart enough to keep quiet lest he too be treated as I was. Remarkable! People, especially but not only religious people, seem to have a deep investment in being able to look down on others who they regard as beyond the reach of decency, truth or even of God. If anyone should claim that these 'enemies' might also be bearers of truth or that they too are loved of God, then that person too can be regarded as guilty of treason in the political world or heresy in the religious world.

Things cut up rough at Nazareth because Jesus gave value to persons, from Sidon and Syria – outsiders, so called enemies of God. He affirmed that God was active within these communities and implied that the essence of God-like love was to reach across boundaries of suspicion and accumulated antagonism in healing ways. His Nazareth neighbours could not imagine life without official enemies. Distrust of those who lived and believed differently gave them their identity. Jesus was offering an identity built on generosity rather than distrust, peace-making rather than antagonism, reconciliation rather than division.

He was consistent in this throughout his ministry. He taught love of enemies, spent time among those on the margins of society and in his teaching used distrusted groups like Samaritans as examples of true faith. He was expelled from the synagogue at Nazareth and was eventually crucified because he challenged the common assumption that we need enemies, scapegoats, people we can look down on, that we are the chosen ones while others live beyond the reach of Divine love. The strange happenings at the synagogue at Nazareth continue to be enacted in our time and place.

Where does all this leave us who are inheritors of the words of Jesus and explorers of the Christ way? First, we can accept that at the heart of the Christian gospel is the simple affirmation that we live in a world where no person or group exists outside of the love of God. Spirit binds us together as a single, though often dysfunctional, human family. It is possible to live without looking down on or denying the essential humanity of those who differ from us in nationality, history, culture or religion. God-spirit is within them as God is within us.

Secondly, Christian life can be understood as an enactment of ancient Jubilee legislation adopted by Jesus as his manifesto. Bringing good news to the poor, proclaiming freedom to captives, freedom to the oppressed and healing to the blind is a good check-list for identifying what we are, or would like to be about, individually and as a congregation. Within the ambiguities of human existence and aware of our own weakness, we can still create fragments of Jubilee existence in a world still wracked by injustice, violence and disregard for the dignity of every person.

Thirdly, we can recognise ourselves to be on a journey towards a life lived without the need of scapegoats, enemies or people who we look down on. It's not a simple pathway to follow and there's a lot of learned prejudice and judgmental attitudes to be overcome. While we have a continuing need to belong to groups where our identity and deepest values are affirmed we also need to guard against falling into the trap of tribalism and the accompanying tendency to look down on those who are different. Jesus at Nazareth affirmed, that Jubilee qualities can be woven into the fabric of human society and that an essential part of that project is learning how to live with a universal and inclusive attitude. But, as with Jesus at Nazareth, don't expect everyone to understand or support you in your efforts.

Exploring Further

Among many excellent books on the Hebrew Sabbath-Jubilee legislation, Sharon H. Ringe, *Jesus, Liberation and the Biblical Jubilee*, 1985, is a good place to start.

BUILDING THE WAY, ON THE WAY

The Way pioneered by Jesus represents a direction, a cluster of questions in search of resolution, possibilities awaiting risky enactment. The Jesus story as outlined in the Gospels describes how Jesus built a pathway into life. He had a sense of direction but the actual deeds and words were crafted on the way. He responded to the needs and questions of those he met, his words were shaped by the circumstances of his time and the events that formed his society. He learned from those he met and built and pioneered a Way that has endured. We too learn on the Way and our teachers are often from unexpected backgrounds.

1

Jesus converted by a Canaanite woman
Matthew 15: 21-28

> As the Jesus story unfolds, we catch glimpses of the Jubilee Way being enacted in the everyday and with a rich variety of characters and groups. Jubilee existence senses the truth within the life of our neighbour, learning from others as the following story demonstrates.

A good way of reading a Biblical text is to look for surprises or unexpected things happening within the world of the story; and there is certainly a surprise at the heart of this reading about Jesus' encounter with a woman from the margins of first-century Palestine.

In each of the four Gospels, Jesus is depicted as pioneering the pathways of God-love in a bruised and divided society and among bruised and divided people. There were things to be learned on the way for Jesus and for the disciple band with which he shared the possibilities and perils of his chosen journey. Jesus was not handed an infallible script from which he was to act and speak as he set out on his way through life. He was more like an improviser, guided by a strong desire to embody God-love and a willingness to live with whatever consequences followed from this choice. So the Gospels are best read by those who have a similar intention and, like him, seek, within the limitations of human weakness, to embody God-love in the society and world where we live.

The big surprise in our story is that the woman clearly comes from left field and is described as a Canaanite. She's the only person in the New Testament explicitly described in this way. Canaanites were the cultural group who lived in Palestine before the Hebrews arrived and from whom the land was stolen. Israelite theologians and political leaders justified this act of genocide and purposeful violence as being the will and purpose of Warrior-God whose larger purpose, they judged, was to provide a land where they could live out their dream. But first they had to get rid of the Canaanites and the way they did that left no room for generosity, justice or compassion, qualities that figured largely in the dream they had inherited from Moses and his interpreters.

By the time of Jesus, there was no specific race or social group described as Canaanites but the word still conjured up thoughts about people who lived on the margin of society, quintessential enemies of Israel, people to be carefully watched and certainly distrusted as enemies of the state and even of God. Words in Deuteronomy 7:1-4 described how the first Canaanites were treated: 'When you enter into your new land, God will clear away many nations before you – you must completely destroy them, make no agreement with them, show no mercy to them, neither should you permit intermarriage with them'. They're words motivated by fear of the stranger, distrust of the other, expressions of personal insecurity and violent aggression while and blasphemously masquerading as 'the will of God'.

In the Gospel, this woman from the edges of Palestinian society speaks for all who are despised, distrusted, swept to the margins of society and who dream of a day when an unjust and unsympathetic society will learn the ways of inclusion, justice and social honesty.

Jesus converted by a Canaanite woman Matthew 15: 21-28

She's heard of Jesus' interest in spiritual and social change in Israel. She's heard of his ministry to the poor among his own people and now she confronts him and challenges him to expand the horizons of his ministry to excluded people of non-Jewish background like her and her daughter. Surely, she thinks, authentic love or mercy knows no national or social boundaries. There's got to be room for everyone in a genuinely just, generous and hospitable society. If Jesus is a genuine pioneer of the shape God-love takes within the human family, then, she surmises, he needs to notice people like her who are labelled differently but whose needs are great and whose wisdom and experience waits to be unwrapped and prized as their special gift to society.

Perhaps she also represents a conviction within the community from which the Gospel of Matthew grew that it's time for Israel – people and politicians, theologians and rabbis – to apologise to those from whom their ancestors had stolen the land while claiming it was a love gift to them from Yahweh. The Gospel of Matthew arose from within the life and reflections of a Jewish-Christian community wrestling with the question as to whether one needed to be a card-carrying Jew to belong to the emerging Jesus Way. Mathew's Gospel is soaked in Jewish imagery but there are hints of a wider horizon: the Gospel begins with a genealogy of Jesus that includes four so-called pagan women; in chapter 8, Jesus heals the servant of a Roman centurion and the Gospel ends with an invitation to go and make disciples of all nations.

But the story of the Canaanite woman has an extra bite to it – this woman challenges Jesus and the way he is still imprisoned by the cultural assumptions of his own birth community – she challenges him to follow the logic of his own words about not judging, doing to others as you'd have them do to you, being doers of truth rather than hearers only, loving enemies, forgiving without limit. She's honest about her need – she has a troubled daughter who she hopes Jesus can heal. But she's more than her daughter's need - she's a person from the margins with a gift to share. Jesus does heal the child but according to the story Jesus is also healed of the racism and bigotry he, like others in his society, took for granted.

The story of the Canaanite woman is a story of Jesus' conversion to a truly universal expression of God-love. The Canaanite woman becomes Jesus' teacher, jolting him into a life-changing awareness that authentic God-love knows no boundaries. It's an obvious truth we need to rediscover, or be found by, over and over for the prejudices of our upbringing and the unspoken assumptions of our culture cling to us like invisible garments.

The role of the Canaanite woman in the unfolding of the Jesus story as told by Matthew is very significant. The inclusive attitudes he learned from her contributed greatly to his reputation as a trouble-maker and so indirectly, one could argue, led to his death at the hands of those for whom God-love was limited to the so-called 'chosen' and socially privileged. Jesus, like the woman, turned the inherited distrust of gentiles on its head. He accepted the socially outrageous suggestion that those on the margin, those who are historically distrusted may have wisdom and experience that we need if we are to continue on our journey into God-love and towards a just and peaceful society. Even 'Canaanites' can be among our teachers and we need their wisdom. Like us, Jesus was on a journey into truth and he learned from others, he respected their wisdom and he valued the experience they shared. How strange that later generations would picture Jesus as a figure who knew everything, needed no one and was born a completed person.

I could continue to explore the Gospel text but we need to return to our day with whatever insights, questions or possibilities are gifted to us in our brief walk around this Gospel story. It's worth staying with the idea that Jesus allows himself to be conquered by the woman. She becomes the teacher and Jesus is the learner – a reversal of how the later church thought of Jesus. Long ago, her people were put to the sword by an army led by Joshua

Jesus converted by a Canaanite woman Matthew 15: 21-28

the celebrated servant of Warrior-God. Now centuries later this un-named woman spiritually conquers Jesus and is the agent of his 'conversion', away from God-love limited to a few and summoning him to the more excellent way of universal, seamless God-love.

Rather than defending his strategy and his inherited prejudices, he listens and allows himself to be conquered by a larger and more generous understanding of God-love. He allows himself to be rescued, by her persistence, from the network of prejudice and scapegoating behaviour, so well represented by the disciples in our story. We are told that the daughter of the woman is tormented by a demon. Is her 'demon' in reality the cruel social handicap inflicted on her as a Canaanite by the intolerant and self-satisfied society in which she and her family live? Before this incident, Jesus is depicted arguing with Pharisees (Matthew 15:1-20) about the finer points of religious law. What a load of nonsense compared with the life and death issues represented by this unnamed woman. While Pharisees argue about whether you should ritually wash your hands before a meal, the woman asks why she and her child are excluded from full participation in their society.

I have never met a Canaanite woman and you probably haven't either but I have met with plenty of people who have questioned me, sometimes explicitly, sometimes indirectly and they've enriched my understanding of life and my appreciation of the seamless nature of God-love. I've learned from some excellent academic teachers over the years but my most important teachers have been those who like the Canaanite woman have challenged me to recognise truth beyond what I think I know and have extended the horizons of God-love within which I and the church of which I'm part seek to live. I think of Tongan and Samoan parishioners from whose experience I deepened my awareness of the dark stream of racism that flows within western culture; of Maori parishioners, colleagues and activists who opened my eyes wider to dark sides of New Zealand history and pushed me into new understandings of the nature of social exclusion. I think of parishioners like Irene, the shy mother living by the Kapuni railway line, Billy the hermit living in a tin shed under Mt Taranaki, each of whom taught me treasured lessons about the nature of Christian ministry; gay, lesbian and trans-gender parishioners who in sharing how they were treated by family, society and church, caused me to extend the horizons of God-love far beyond what church courts at that time could tolerate.

I recall Muslim, Jewish, Buddhist and Hindu friends from whom I have learned so much about life in God. And so on... how about you? Have you met with metaphorical 'Canaanites' who have jolted you into deepening faith, broadened your understanding of life and of the boundary breaking-nature of God-love? They're a gift to be treasured. They're all around us if we meet them, listen to them and weave their wisdom into our living.

Exploring Further

> There are plenty of books that describe how women and 'culturally different' people have been excluded or whose lives have been diminished by church members over the centuries A recent American book by Jeannine Hill Fletcher, *The sin of white supremacy – Christianity, Racism and religious diversity in America*, 2017, describes how white male supremacy and the rarely recognised assumptions behind it have scarred humanity and diminished the lives of those excluded, caricatured or not taken seriously. It's an ugly story.

2

A world without scapegoats?

Luke 9:51-62

> Over and over, we find that the Bible and in this case the Jesus Books are dealing with issues that continue to mislead humanity – like the theme of this sermon.

Today's Gospel reading has important wisdom to share with us as we seek the way of Jesus in a challenging world.

The story is simple. Jesus is on his way to Jerusalem. We know that it will be his last journey and that when he arrives at the great city, guardians of a political, economic and religious system that is living on borrowed time, will kill him. The days of ministry in Galilee, when he moved among the poor, marginalised and the needy of that area, are being left behind. Jesus now has business to attend to in Jerusalem. Conflict had surrounded his work in Galilee where he consistently offended those who were guardians and beneficiaries of the status quo. In Jerusalem the level of conflict will be multiplied greatly when he confronts the powerful of the capital city.

In travelling from Galilee to Jerusalem, Jesus and the pilgrim band of which he and his disciples were part needed to pass through the area of Samaria. Some teachers said it was better to travel around, rather than through, Samaria because it was regarded as 'unclean' territory. Jesus and his disciples would have been taught from childhood to distrust Samaritans who were regarded as traitorous half-breeds whose ancestors had failed the nation in its hour of need.

Seven hundred years earlier, when many of the leaders of Israel were taken into captivity in Babylon the 'nobodies' of Samaria were left behind. It was said that they did nothing to preserve the traditions of their people and instead fell into the religious ways of unbelievers. When the natural leaders of the nation finally returned from Babylon and set about rebuilding Jerusalem and re-establishing the faith of their ancestors, their plans were resented by the Samaritans who refused to cooperate and actively opposed the rebuilding of the Temple and the city walls. They erected a rival temple on Mount Gerizim and reduced the Holy Scriptures only to the first five books. To add to their betrayal, they were also regarded as overly friendly toward Greek and Roman overlords.

Distrust of Samaritans was part of the political air that people breathed. Life for Jews was tough enough under Roman occupation without having to be troubled by internal divisions and betrayals. In a time of national fragility and division, people looked around for someone to blame for their plight. The Samaritans were an obvious target. They had failed the nation before; their beliefs were not mainstream and they were in bed with the Romans. I assume that the suggestion of the disciples in verse 54 that Jesus might cause fire to come upon an inhospitable Samaritan village is a metaphorical way of suggesting that they might treat them as badly as their behaviour deserved. They were only suggesting what they had been taught to imagine since they were children. The Samaritans were a ready scapegoat on whose heads the nation's anger, disappointment and sense of betrayal could be loaded.

A world without scapegoats? Luke 9:51-62

Scapegoating is an old and well-worn strategy. The anger, uncertainty and disappointments of a society are poured onto a scapegoat – a person or group who could be blamed for anything and everything that has gone wrong. The title comes from the ancient Israelite custom recorded in Leviticus 6 when hands were laid on a goat, representing the transmission of the sin of the community to the scapegoat who was then banished into the wilderness. The people then got on with life, free from the burden of their own shortcomings. René Girard, a French intellectual who studied the phenomena of scapegoating, suggested that human culture is based on the ancient and violent practice of scapegoating. Societies that are otherwise divided by disagreement and failure achieve a form of negative unity through their shared opposition to the scapegoat.

Humans are by nature a competitive and violent lot. Conflict is never far away and the disintegration of society is an ever-present possibility. In choosing a person or group to be a scapegoat conflicts that emerge from human error and shortcomings, that we all share in and that could destroy society, are projected onto the scapegoat. The community is saved from destructive violence as human violence is deflected onto the scapegoat. Persecution of the scapegoat means the community receives the gift of unity and peace as potential enemies are united in shared hatred of the common enemy – the scapegoat. Because the act of scapegoating brings unity to an otherwise divided community the idea grew that in pouring communal anger upon a scape-goat, be it an individual or a group, this violent behaviour was a way of serving God's will which, after all, is the creation of unity within the human family.

There are plenty of Biblical tales of scapegoating. The most notable for Christians is reflected in the words of High Priest Caiaphas (John 18:14) who when consulted about what should be done with Jesus replied, 'It is better to have one person die for the people'. Through the death of this preacher of God's love, conflict between various groups in Israel would be avoided or at least delayed. The list of those who have played the part of scapegoat in western history, usually with the blessing of the church, makes dreary and shameful reading: The Jews, described as Christ killers; people with black or dark skin who were treated shamefully; homosexuals who were regarded as contaminated; gypsies whose wandering ways were distrusted; migrants, refugees and adherents of other religions whose difference was regarded as an affront to God's plans. The church has read the words of the disciples, 'shall we bring fire upon these Samaritans', shall we perpetuate their role as scapegoats, shall we continue to paper over the cracks in our society and create artificial unity built upon our shared hatred of these wretches but we have not heeded the response of Jesus when he rebuked the disciples for their knee-jerk acceptance of scapegoating as though it was condoned by God-love.

The organised church has often engaged in scapegoating in its own life, buying a form of unity among the majority by focusing aggression against a minority group or an individual who disagrees with the party line. Heretics, who have questioned orthodoxy, have been put to death or marginalised. The fragile unity of the church has been preserved by violent means. In our day Fundamentalists and Liberals, Evangelicals and Progressives each scapegoat the other, claiming their opponent to be the cause of the church's problems in a secular society. The strange thing is that each group needs the other for they frequently define themselves by their opposition to the other. The question 'Who are you?' is answered: 'Well, we're not them!'

Politicians in every age have known that a sure fire pathway to popularity and power is through identifying a scapegoat and creating a sort of consensus, a rough unity in society, based on opposition towards the person or group so targeted. I recall elections when we were warned about reds under the bed. Now it's Muslims under a burka, or terrorists holding a Qur'an. (George Bush and Osama Bin Laden were a mirror image of each other – each needed the other as a scapegoat as they gathered support for their political ambitions.) So called 'dole bludgers' along with refugees and migrants are commonplace scapegoats chosen by politicians desperate for power. When we next have an election, I wonder who will be scapegoated in the competition for votes? We often puzzle over the strange link between violence and religions that claim to walk the pathway of love. As long as religious people and religious institutions remain captive to forms of scapegoating, we will be forever linked with violence.

In rebuking the disciples for their desire to act violently toward the Samaritan scapegoats, Jesus challenged the scapegoating strategy as a pathway to peace and unity. In rejecting the deep-seated enmity towards Samaritans, he was pointing to another way towards the unity of God's people. Jesus was consistent in his attitude to the Samaritans. He told a parable about an impossibly 'good' Samaritan and a story is told of how he healed ten lepers and only one, a Samaritan, expressed gratitude for his healing. The scapegoating violence proposed by the disciples was a challenge to the main thrust of Jesus' ministry. He consistently gathered the victims of human prejudice, the sick the poor, prisoners, the morally mistaken, foreigners and strangers, into a new community he called the Kingdom of God. Through his acts of hospitality, forgiveness and non-violence, Jesus was initiating a revolution in human living. He was dismantling the scapegoating pathway to spurious peace. Scapegoating is, after all, simply a form of socially sanctioned violence.

We are told that Jesus had set his face to go to Jerusalem. There he will become the scapegoat, the victim of the system's search for power. He will become a scapegoat just like the Samaritans and every victim of the scapegoating mechanism before or since. His death will be a dramatic enactment of the deep truth that God is present with and in the suffering of all victims. His death will become God's invitation to reject the violence of scapegoating and the culture of death that goes with it. There is another way of ordering society and creating the unity we all yearn for. It is the pathway of patient and persistent breaking down of barriers that divide the human community and bearing the pain and cost involved in such action.

The disciples in our passage didn't get it. They couldn't imagine a society without the violence of scapegoating. It was not till after the death and resurrection of Jesus that some of them grasped the radical non-violent alternative and identification with victims that Jesus had proclaimed and embodied. From them and their sensitivity to this alternative way the church was born – a people developing the mind that was in Christ, rejecting the violent foundations on which society was built, standing alongside society's victims and sharing in the creation of a hospitable, generous, forgiving and love-soaked society. Some followed the new path but for others the destructive byways of scapegoating have continued to be seductive.

Exploring Further

Among the many books by and about Girard, those of James Alison represent an excellent introduction. In a series of books, he draws on Girard's wisdom: *Faith beyond resentment*, 2001, *The joy of being wrong*, 1998, *Raising Abel*, 1996. Writing from within the pain of his own experiences of exclusion, he travels from anger to love.

3

The prophet and the centurion

Luke 7:1-10

> Jesus was not sent from some faraway place with a memorised message that could be dropped into the mind and will of every person he met. His message, his ministry, grew from real encounters with real people. His truth was born out of sensitivity to God-love, reflection on his times and in conversation with the people he met.

Today's Gospel reading was sufficiently valued in the early church to be included in three of the four Gospels that made it into the New Testament. (See also Matthew 5:8-13 and John 4:44-54). If a Jesus story is present in more than one Gospel, it's usually cause to pay special attention to it. We have no way of knowing the details of what exactly took place on the occasion when Jesus received a request from a Roman centurion but we can hazard an educated guess as to why the story was treasured and repeated in the early church. That's an important step on the way toward allowing ourselves to be questioned by what we read.

Luke's Gospel almost certainly grew out of the ongoing life of Christian communities in the city of Antioch in northern Syria during the middle years of the first century. It was in Antioch that the Christian movement moved from its origins as a village movement in rural Galilee and became an urban and multicultural movement. It was a cradle from which Christianity, as we know it, was born. Luke claimed it was in Antioch that the disciples were first called 'Christians' (Acts 11: 26). I'm reminded of a story told me by the late Bishop Gibran, Antiochene Orthodox Bishop for Australia and New Zealand. An earnest American Protestant woman was interested to learn he came from Antioch and asked in a Texan accent which American Missionary Society had planted the church in his homeland. 'Madam', he replied, 'it all began with us'.

In Galilee, as in Jerusalem, the emerging church was held within the warm embrace of Jewish custom and ritual. When an outpost of the Jerusalem church was established in urban Antioch, new ways of being people of the Jesus way had to be born – ways more suited to a multi-cultural, socially diverse and multi-religious environment. Gentiles, owing nothing to and knowing little of Jewish custom sought membership of the church in Antioch and contributed to fresh expressions of the way that had attracted them. The urban and cosmopolitan setting of Antioch transformed a Jewish renewal movement built around the memory of Jesus and began the development of a distinctive 'Christian' identity. The apostle Paul, who planted Christian communities in the great cities of the Empire, got his first lessons in urbanised cosmopolitan Christianity during his time in Antioch.

Luke, a spirit-sensitive and literary genius, assembled and edited a 'Jesus Book' to support and guide house churches in their ongoing exploration of what it meant to follow the Jesus way in a new setting. He carefully chose incidents and teachings from the ministry of Jesus that might help the Christians of Antioch in their walk into unexplored territory. He chose incidents and characters

The prophet and the centurion Luke 7:1-10

that readers or hearers could readily identify with. Stories of the poor and homeless sharing meals with Jesus, of women being treated with uncommon respect, of the sick, lonely and left behind being gathered into a new community where compassion reigned, acted as mirrors in which members of the Antioch church could see themselves.

They came from a variety of backgrounds and it was reassuring to hear how people like them were welcomed and valued by Jesus. Former Samaritans gladly heard of how Jesus recognised the neighbourly love of one of their forebears. Luke's Jesus book was like a photo album in which church members found dramatised sketches of their sort of people. They were assured of their place in the church community for whom Jesus was both founder and living presence. Even Jewish teachers who had disagreed with Jesus but were now exploring his Way would have valued stories of him arguing with, eating with and accepting Scribes and Pharisees as persons to be taken seriously.

The story of the Roman Centurion and his ailing servant fits uneasily into Luke's 'Jesus Book'. In other healing stories, Jesus is more intimately engaged with those who seek his help while here he converses and heals from a distance. Is the story about an ailing slave or about a Centurion inconvenienced by the illness of someone whose hard work he depended on? In other healing stories, Jesus reaches out to those living on the margins of society, he has a special care for the overlooked in society. But the Centurion is a man of power and social significance. He's part of an occupying army. He wears the uniform and bears weapons of war. He differs enormously from the non-violent and justice-seeking pathways Jesus pointed towards.

Jewish Elders appreciated his generosity but a question remained as to how the Centurion had made his money. Was it wealth gained through the exploitation of the poor whose taxes he collected on behalf of a far distant Emperor? If he was such a good and kind man, why didn't he leave the army and all it represented? To add to it all he was a slave owner, which meant he lived from the work of Palestinians who had lost their ancestral land to Roman entrepreneurs.

The Christians in Antioch would, I suspect, have been stunned by Luke's decision to include this sympathetic portrayal of a Centurion in his 'Jesus Book'. Jesus had been condemned to death by Roman leaders and Roman soldiers crucified him. Some would have been in Jerusalem during the Jewish rebellion of the 60s when thousands were killed and Roman soldiers destroyed the Temple. So, why include this story of a Roman soldier in the community's 'Jesus Book'?

One clue is that in the preceding chapter Jesus invited his disciples to learn to love their enemies. There's little doubt a Roman centurion could be described as an 'enemy'. A conspicuous military presence never feels friendly to those against whom its suspicions and arms are directed. The inclusion of this story might have been Luke's way of posing the question: is the forgiveness of enemies really possible or is it, as a twentieth-century theologian suggested, 'an impossible possibility'? Perhaps the question could be rephrased: can compassion after the manner of Jesus overcome the fear, hatred and distrust we feel in the presence of those who might harm us? Are there limits to Christian love or is the forgiveness Jesus showed to his tormentors something we can emulate? Can what we have in common with those we disagree with on important matters outweigh our differences? So, those who read or heard Luke's 'Jesus Book', at first puzzled by the inclusion of the Centurion with a sick servant, were left with questions about the relevance or irrelevance of love in the presence of those described as 'enemies'. Is it possible for 'enemies' to meet as neighbours, people subject to the same human weaknesses and struggles?

As we read the Gospel of Luke, we're soon struck by the way the ministry of Jesus is dominated by his interest in the poor and needy. We intuitively admire his care for the poor just as we admire

The prophet and the centurion Luke 7:1-10

those who across the centuries have walked on the same path – St Francis, John Wesley, William Booth and the Salvation Army, the Vincent de Paul Society, City Missions and prophetic figures who call upon governments to attend, on our behalf, to the needs of the most vulnerable. But is Christian ministry and mission solely a reaching out toward the needs of the poor and vulnerable? This may be the essential focus but is it the whole? Is there also a ministry to the powerful, those who make the rules that govern society, whose economic and political decisions and actions have a direct bearing on the well-being of those who are most vulnerable?

I recall when we lived in New York while I was studying at Union Theological Seminary that while many white students looked forward to ministry among the deprived in the city, Afro-American professors were encouraging them to undertake tough and demanding prophetic ministry in white suburbs among the decision-makers of the city where they might help change the pictures in the minds and hearts of those whose daily decisions directly and indirectly affected the lives of the poorest. By his addition of the Centurion story Luke is perhaps commending a ministry to the strong and to those who make the decisions that shape society. In every society, it's the bankers, politicians, industrialists, planners, sometimes military leaders and police, who shape society and indirectly and directly affect the fortunes of those who are vulnerable and easily damaged by unwise or uncaring decisions.

Luke describes how Jesus drew a Centurion into his orbit, presumably to help him change so he might become a builder rather than a destroyer of human community, a builder of peace rather than conflict, a sharer rather than a taker. My experience is that beyond the swagger and apparent confidence of the so-called 'strong' there are the same insecurities, inner battles, unresolved grief and silly mistakes that we all share as part of our human condition – whether you live in a ghetto of the wealthy or a ghetto of the poor. Alongside a care for the poor and needy, we might also ask how we might help those in positions of power over others to develop values and ethical perspectives that can guide their decision-making into ways that will benefit the whole community. Is there a specific ministry to the powerful and the so called strong – to people like the Centurion?

If I had written Luke's story of the Centurion with the ailing servant, I'd have concluded it differently. The Centurion would have ripped off his uniform, thrown away whatever weapons he had and given a letter of release to each of the slaves who had so faithfully served his needs. He'd have purchased land for each of them, sufficient to keep their families in relative comfort, and then set up a 'Free the slaves' movement in Antioch. But that's not the way Luke finished the story. He did, however, in a later chapter, include a story about a tax collector, Zacchaeus, who overcame his chronic addiction to affluence and returned what he'd taken from others through lawful but unethical practices (Luke 18:18-30). Fortunately Luke was smarter than me; he just left questions for the folks at Antioch and folks like us to chew over. One last question: who is most in need of healing in the story – the sick slave or the Centurion locked into a system that so dominated his life that he'd become simply a cog in a great imperial system?

Exploring Further

Among the many books available on the political, economic and social context in which Jesus lived and for which the Gospels were written, I have been particularly helped by the work of Richard Horsley. In *The Message and the Kingdom*, 1997, he summarises some of his more detailed study and also includes the life and work of Paul and his communities.

4

A prophet of the new order

Luke 7:36-50

> Jesus was killed because he refused to be captured by ways of living that, though popular with the wealthy, meant death or poverty for the poor. He was a prophet of a new order, he named the defects in what was and reached forward to a new world.

I'm often embarrassed, as I'm sure you are, by the public perception of the Christian church. We're frequently portrayed in media and in conversation as moralistic critics of those whose lives fall below our standards of middle class morality. Statements by church spokespersons often come across as judgmental, moralistic and exclusionary. It's easy to point the finger at others and decry their judgmental and moralistic attitudes but it's an easy pattern to fall into and probably none of us escape entirely from the dangerous net of moral superiority, a tendency to look down on those who have tripped up along the journey of life. There's wisdom in the words about leaving it to those who are without sin to cast the first stone! The reality is we're all caught up in the business of putting a life together and, for some, that's a tougher ride than for others. We need to be careful if we throw moral stones.

The issue of how to live a moral Christian life without lapsing into judgmental attitudes towards those who seem to us to be morally crippled is not a new issue. It's the background question behind today's gospel reading, the story of Jesus who forgives, Simon who judges and an unnamed woman who expresses gratitude. The story, which is found in slightly different forms in each of the Gospels, takes us near to the heart of Luke's depiction of the new way pioneered by Jesus.

The story is simple. There was a rumour in the villages of Galilee that Jesus, the preacher from Nazareth, was claiming to be a prophet – a successor of those who in past generations had boldly declared the will of God for their time. Then, as now, there were plenty of preachers, social commentators and politicians claiming to represent final truth. Jewish teachers made a distinction between true and false prophets, though a decision as to who was true and who was false tended to depend on the interests and ambitions of the person making the judgment. Simon, a Pharisee and guardian of religious conformity, decided to find out what sort of prophet Jesus is – true or false, authentic or charlatan? His question turned around and bit him where it hurts most – in his precious sense of moral superiority.

In the story, two ways of living are set out that lie at the heart of the conflict in Luke's telling of the Jesus story. Simon's attitude towards Jesus is shaped by suspicion and the harshness of dogmatic moral certainty. The woman's attitude towards Jesus is shaped by gratitude and disregard for normal social propriety. Simon's suspicion that Jesus is probably a fraud, a false prophet or foolish trouble-maker, is clear in Luke's telling of the story. In welcoming Jesus, Simon omits all the normal and culturally appropriate courtesies. There's no kiss of greeting, no washing of feet and hands. It was a privilege in that society to host a teacher or rabbi but, though Simon later refers to Jesus as 'teacher', he fails to welcome him with the appropriate rituals. So he declares his doubts about Jesus even before mealtime conversation has begun. Perhaps he intends to humiliate Jesus.

The appearance of a woman, perhaps known already to other guests, who enters the open house to express gratitude to Jesus, is a conversation stopper. It seems she had met Jesus before and had been welcomed by him with respect and acceptance. It may be significant that she is unnamed. She's not regarded as a person. She's labelled as 'sinner', part of an ill-defined but discriminated against group. A tradition developed that she was a prostitute but Luke doesn't tell us that.

The woman's treatment of Jesus is extravagant and counter-cultural. Observing Simon's inadequate welcome to Jesus, she goes overboard. Simon's mean-spirited attitudes are shown up by her embarrassingly personalised actions – perfume, kisses and tears for his feet and to top it all off she wipes his feet with her hair. Each of her actions has symbolic significance. Mark tells the same story and suggests the washing with perfume is a premonition of his death and anointing. Kenneth Bailey, a scholar who spent a lifetime living and working in the Middle East suggests the woman's tears are not for her forgiven shortcomings but for Jesus' public humiliation at the hands of Simon. She is in anguish because, this beautiful person who set her free with a message of the love of God for sinners, is being publicly humiliated. She is identifying with Jesus who has been treated badly by a person of privilege who should know better. The gifts and actions of our woman remind us of the extravagant gifts brought to the infant Jesus by foreign teachers in Matthew's dramatic birth story.

Bailey observes that though only the woman is described as a 'sinner' in reality the room was occupied by two types of sinners: law keeper sinners like Simon and law breaker sinners like the woman. As a law keeper, Simon could quote chapter and verse to confirm the woman's shortcomings. Law-bound people like Simon can always find reasons to justify their judgmental ways. Bailey includes some wonderful quotes from rabbis regarding how sinful it was for a woman to go out with her hair unbound in the manner of this woman. A second century rabbi talked about a man's religious duty to divorce a wife who goes into the street with hair unfastened and with her armpits uncovered! Even today, in some Middle Eastern countries, a woman's hair is considered sexually provocative and hence a trap for weak men. Bailey notes that a recent Iranian Prime Minister, Rafsanjani, claimed 'It is the obligation of the female to cover her head because women's hair exudes vibrations that arouse, excite, mislead, and corrupt men!!'

These culturally-shaped practices, today identified with sections of Islam alone, have deep roots in the cultures from which Biblical religion was born. It's worth repeating these references if only to demonstrate how moral codes differ between different cultural or national groups. So bound up is Simon with his notions of good and evil, law and sin, that he feels entirely justified in dismissing the woman as a worthless sinner. He knew Biblical passages that encouraged love for neighbour and for strangers – but as we know, when a seriously righteous moralist gets going, notions of love, forgiveness and possibility are quickly forgotten.

Verse 39 is central in the story: When Simon the Pharisee saw the actions of the woman, he said to himself, 'If this man were a prophet he'd have known what kind of woman this is who is touching him – that she is a sinner'. The irony is that Jesus is a prophet and he knows about the woman's failures. That's why he accepts her. He's a prophet of a new order of existence. Simon belongs to the old order and cannot understand Jesus' acceptance of the woman and her rule breaking. The Kingdom within which Simon lives is narrow, judgmental and harsh. Jesus is prophet of a more expansive, compassionate and inclusive way of life. Who is the greater sinner in the parable? We assume the woman is the 500 denarii sinner and that Simon is a far more modest wrongdoer. It seems to me that much more harm has been done across the centuries, and is still done, by the harsh guardians of unforgiving moralism. The damage they inflict on the already handicapped or marginalised is vast.

Quite simply, Jesus tells Simon that the woman he has labelled 'bad' is in his eyes more sensitive to life and its possibilities than Simon, the moral vulture. While the woman fills the house with overflowing acceptance and joy, Simon offers only judgment, criticism and put-down labelling. The story may be received as a warning to us to be cautious in viewing and assessing others through the filters of our inherited and culturally shaped moral standards. A new moral standard is born with Jesus and that is compassion and understanding. Compassion enables us to see real people, their needs, their struggles, their possibilities; and questions the human tendency to label them as 'sinner', or as part of whatever cultural, national or religious group is the current scapegoat. I suspect we've all got a bit of Simon in us. It's part of the middle class and, dare I say, churchy air we breathe. According to today's reading we may be drifting from the pathway pioneered by Jesus if these attitudes are allowed to grow unchecked. The story of Jesus the forgiver, the unnamed 'sinner' woman and Simon the prisoner of his own moralism is an important reminder of the new order of existence lived and taught by Jesus.

In reading this story, I was reminded of a time I preached on it about fifty years ago. My sermon had three points: in those days all sermons had three points, and I focused on the three words of Jesus to the woman: 'Your sins are forgiven'; 'your faith has saved you'; 'go in peace'. During the week, two strangers present in the service came to visit me. They had come to church on a whim, seeking something needed but not easily defined. Life was an uphill struggle for them and they'd made mistakes. I still recall their words: 'We didn't feel judged, we felt valued by you and those we spoke with after the service'. I never saw them again for they lived in a different part of New Zealand. But 'gospel' happened that Sunday morning. Just imagine if every needy person who entered a church or met a Christian person, in any setting, could say the same thing: 'I didn't feel judged, I felt valued'.

'Do not neglect to show hospitality to strangers, for by so doing some have entertained angels without knowing it.' (Hebrews 13:2)

Exploring Further

The best book I know on forgiveness is written by theologian, L. Gregory Jones: *Embodying Forgiveness, A theological analysis*, 1995. Forgiveness is central to a way of life that no longer needs to condemn others, that accepts our own weakness and the weakness of others, that values community over revenge, is a way of living, our human participation in the love of God. Should churches be offering courses on 'Living into forgiveness'? Desmond Tutu said, 'Without forgiveness, there is no future'. Donald Shriver, *An Ethic for Enemies*, 1995, explores forgiveness in politics.

STEWARDS OF THE WAY PIONEERED BY JESUS

If the way of Jesus is to be available for future generations, there will need to be some sort of community dedicated to the task of making his wisdom, spiritual depth and social vision available as humanity builds new futures.

The Way pioneered by Jesus was treasured in first-century communities of people dedicated to exploring and living the Jesus Way in their village, town or city. Initially passed on by word of mouth, memorised and recited in their weekly gathering his words and deeds were eventually written down so they could be shared with those who enquired about what and who motivated the followers of the Way.

The four Gospels differ for they arose within and served the needs of different communities or cluster of house churches. Each treasured particular memories of Jesus that helped them in their desire to follow in the Way of living he pioneered. As they heard, explored and discussed these words, they felt they were in touch with the living Jesus. It was as though they were in conversation with him and with the truth he lived.

It is often the same with us – we read the words, we puzzle over them, we allow them to question us, our minds leap ahead asking what it might mean for us if we were to live within this wisdom, this lifestyle, this horizon. As we continue to meditate on what we have read, it is as though we are in conversation with the man who first spoke these words. The words we have read begin to mean more than *when they were first spoken and remembered. They are spoken to us and into our world.*

The words and deeds of Jesus, written and interpreted in the Gospels and received by subsequent generations of readers, represent deep and life-transforming wisdom. They are a doorway into a style of living greatly needed in our troubled times. Note that this sort of 'deep truth' is not dependant on historical accuracy. It doesn't matter that there are historical differences between the four Gospels and some of the Jesus stories seem to represent a form of what might be called poetic, imaginative or embellished memory. 'Embellished memory' is a feature of most transformative story-telling and there's plenty of it in the Biblical writings – a sort of stylised and widely understood form of spiritual exaggeration, hyperbole, a style of ancient writing, which claims our attention, our imagination and opens us to new possibilities.

Transforming truth is conveyed in stories that question and summon us to ways of living that enhance rather than damage human community. The church is true to it's deepest self when it's 'a community of the questioned ones', allowing ourselves to be continually questioned by the words and deeds of Jesus. We don't have the answers to every question but we do have a starting point that we return to over and over.

1

Stewards of the words of Jesus

John 17:8

> The time when the words of Jesus were widely known, sometimes memorised and often quoted in public discourse is over. It seems to me we are losing contact with a storehouse of questioning wisdom with its capacity to jolt us into new ways of living, alert us to deep mystery at the heart of life and point us toward healing possibilities for our lives and the life of our communities.

As I read our gospel reading, a part of the final prayer John imagined Jesus praying with his disciples before his death, the words of verse 8 jumped out at me and claimed a role in today's worship. This is Jesus speaking to God in prayer: 'The words that you gave to me I have given to them (i.e. the disciples), and they have received them and know in truth that I come from you' (John 17:8).

The Gospel of John is an extended reflection on the significance of Jesus and was written about 60 or 70 years after his death. It tells us as much about the infant church and how Jesus was regarded in the churches of Asia Minor as it tells us about the historical Jesus of Palestine. The words of verse 8, 'the words that you gave to me I have given to them' offer us a fresh, and, I think, important, description of the church as 'Stewards of the Words of Jesus'. The church can be understood as the community who received the words of Jesus and who continue to share and to explore these words on behalf of, and with, the whole human family.

The words and wisdom of Jesus arose from within his sensitivity to God and to the possibilities he saw for lives lived within the purposes of God. His words emerged from within a life more thoroughly and consistently sensitive to the will of God than any other person we're in touch with. They're words that should not be lost to the human family. His words are among the most precious treasures of humanity.

The author of John's Gospel was interested in describing how the influence of Jesus might continue into what he sensed would be an insecure and uncertain future. Like the other Gospel writers, he wanted to ensure that the revolution in human living begun by Jesus would continue and shape future generations. So John identifies two ways through which Jesus will be experienced as a lively and transforming presence. The first is that the Spirit of God will goad and comfort, strengthen and lead the Jesus community into whatever the future brings. The second is that there will be a group who will be stewards, or reminders to humanity, of the words of Jesus. This will be a community where the words of Jesus are received as doorways into the mystery of life and into God-love. Members of this community deliberately live into and from the words of Jesus. At their best they become embodiments and reminders of the wisdom of Jesus within the ambiguities of human history.

We should be troubled that the words of Jesus are neither well-known nor heeded in our secular society. As stewards of these words, we have a responsibility to ensure they remain available to our culture in a time when many flounder about for a direction to life's adventure. The words of Jesus do not provide neat answers to all our questions. Their power, as recorded in the Gospels, is their capacity to jolt readers into new ways of seeing and living life. The words of Jesus consistently question inherited assumptions and attitudes we take for granted. They place a question mark alongside values and ways of doing things that everyone assumes are right and proper.

We take it for granted that war is an inevitable part of human living but we read that Jesus said 'Blessed are the peacemakers for they shall be called the children of God'. We live in a world were it seems to be taken for granted that starvation is a natural occurrence within some nations and regions of the earth, that prisoners and the needy beyond our own community are someone else's problem. Jesus pictured God saying 'I was hungry and you gave me food, I was thirsty and you gave me something to drink, I was a stranger and you welcomed me, I was naked and you gave me clothing, I was sick and you took care of me, I was in prison and you visited me'.

In a world where revenge has become an art form and grudges are allowed to linger, Jesus, in response to a question replied that his disciples should forgive without limit—even seventy times seven! We could go on quoting from the imaginative and forceful, disorienting and challenging words of Jesus. Sometimes, Jesus' words are puzzling yet tantalising in their invitation to explore new ways of living. For instance, try this: 'Those who want to save their life will lose it, and those who lose their life for my sake and for the sake of the gospel, will save it. For what will it profit them to gain the whole world and forfeit their life?' These are words to live with, to meditate on, to pray into, till something of their wisdom seeps into everyday living.

The words of Jesus could not be enshrined in law or regulations. They're not that sort of wisdom. The words of Jesus, in parable, sayings and proverbs, typically cause hearers and readers to stop and think again about actions they take for granted but that fall short of genuinely healing truth. Jesus called into being a community who were distinctive, not because they were smarter than others, but because they were open to new possibilities and were willing to be questioned by the way Jesus lived and spoke. Put it this way: We know very little. We live on small islands of certainty surrounded by a great sea of mystery and uncertainty. The words of Jesus, if we will enter into their world, take us towards the edge of what we are comfortable with, to the edge of our small island, and invite us to imagine another way to the way we currently live. The words of Jesus are unsettling. They speak of possibilities of sharing with others, forgiving enemies, welcoming strangers, caring for the marginalised, trusting in Divine grace to guide us through life's tough places.

No one will ever be able to write a definitive description of the meaning of the words of Jesus. They mean more than the Gospel writers intended, they carry more meaning than even Jesus knew. They come alive in surprising and transforming ways in every generation and in every place. The meaning of Jesus' words as edited by the Gospel writers is never exhausted. Like dry leaves they can catch fire and come alive in fresh ways as people wanting to live life well study, explore and enact what they find in these words.

There is recognition in John 17 that those to whom the words of Jesus have been given should not expect to be well received by the world. The church's task is to share Jesus' words with the world but, though the world may need this wisdom, there is an inbuilt resistance. The word 'world' is used in two senses in John. The first refers to the world as the natural and human community that is loved of God (John 3:16). In this passage, 'world' refers to the systems and ideologies of the world community that serve to derail the human adventure, deny the possibilities of peace, justice, sharing and forgiveness.

Paul describes these same systems as 'Principalities and Powers'. These are the political, economic, religious and cultural practices that though taken for granted do not necessarily serve the purposes of God. When in verse 11 Jesus says he is no longer in the world it is a statement of fact. The systems that claim to rule life find no room for the unpredictability and challenge of the somewhat freewheeling yet life-enhancing perspectives found in the words of Jesus. When in v.14 Jesus says that the world hates the church because it does not belong to the system, John is drawing attention to something that could be seen and experienced in his day. Governments and leaders were becoming aware of the counter-cultural tendencies found in the communities who understood themselves to be stewards of the words of Jesus.

By the end of the first century, Christians were becoming marginalised as troublemakers who wanted to change the Roman Empire. They were troublemakers who questioned the way things were, in the light of the new possibilities for human living found in the words of Jesus. Sadly, the later church dealt with this rejection by the system by smoothing down the rough edges of the words of Jesus so they would no longer offend those locked into the ways of the systems that controlled them and their communities. That was a tragic time for the Christian adventure and it's not yet over.

In some Protestant churches, a Bible is processed in at the commencement of worship. The words of Jesus with all their challenge, questioning and possibilities for our lives and for the life of our world are brought in and become a focus for our time together. During the week, we live within the script given to us by a secularised system that finds little room for acknowledgment of the words and perspectives of Jesus. We live amid half-truths and compromises, we see and read of violence and injustice, the great god 'greed' stalks us all. It would be easy for us to be taken over by this system that, though legal, is more a servant of death than of life.

On Sunday morning, we gather around the words of Jesus again, recognise our role as stewards of these words and, most importantly, through prayer, meditation, thinking and imaginative listening, place our lives yet again within the horizon of the words. In terms of the systems of our day, what we do is like an act of disobedience. We declare we will not be controlled by the systems of our time. We march to another tune. I am reminded of what Jewish teacher Martin Buber said to Gestapo troopers when he was asked if he had any seditious literature in his house. 'Yes', he said, 'I have a Bible.' We might say to such a question: 'Yes and we are stewards of the dangerous and revolutionary words of Jesus'.

The words of Jesus are our primary point of contact with the living Christ. As we read, ponder, question, study and argue with these words in the Gospels we often find we are drawn more deeply into our own lives and into the life of God. As we feel the challenge of what we read, it sometimes seems we are in conversation with Jesus himself. The words of Jesus are more than another bit of 'stuff' to add onto the outside of our life. They're more like a dynamic that changes us and our communities from the inside out. As stewards of the words of Jesus, our high destiny within the purposes of God is to allow those words to so soak into our living that we might become reflections of the living Christ in our time.

As churches, we have the responsibility of ensuring that the words of Jesus, the new possibilities for living found in those words, the questions addressed to humanity through those words, are heard in our time and place. I do not know in detail how we can best incorporate the words of Jesus into contemporary Western living but I do know those words are still needed and we need to plot and plan how we, along with others, can infiltrate society with the revolutionary words of Jesus.

Exploring Further

Two books, Robert Tannehill, *The Sword of his Mouth* (1975) and Amos Niven Wilder, *Early Christian Rhetoric*

– *the Language of the Gospel*, (1964), first alerted me to how the language and literary forms used by the Gospel writers helped to shape the message they share. It is language that invites participation in the questions and possibilities of what is spoken of. It conveys more than barren facts – it invites readers to stop, consider, reflect, imagine, choose. It is language that draws us into a conversation with possibilities for contemporary living, believing and hoping. Imaginative participation in what is read is the key to understanding deep truth. Wilder memorably wrote: 'Before the message there must be the vision; before the sermon the hymn; before the prose the poem'.

2

Refusing to serve an unjust system
Matthew 25:14-30

> The parables of Jesus take us deep into the message and teaching style of Jesus. They are imaginative narratives with a catch in the tail that challenge us to imagine fresh ways of putting life together, questioning things we take for granted. The tragedy is that over the centuries the sharp and challenging edges of the parables have been worn down and they have been reduced to common sense and socially acceptable decency.
>
> Among the contemporary writers who have done most to recover the challenge implicit in the parables is William Herzog. I am dependant upon his re-interpretation of a well-known parable in what follows. I make no apologies for leaning on his work for it deserves to be more widely known.

The more I study and meditate on the Gospel parables, the more I become aware of the radical nature of the Jesus way. Over the centuries the questioning edges of the parables have been worn down, domesticated, by preachers and writers unwilling or unable to hear the challenge within these simple narratives. When we set Jesus in his first-century setting, we find that many of our traditional interpretations of Gospel passages fall far short of the revolutionary way pioneered by Jesus.

Today's Parable of the Talents is such a passage. The popular interpretation that finds in the parable an invitation to invest our talents, our natural abilities, our gifts, in projects that reap the best rewards for ourselves and our masters is not so much wrong because parables can have many meanings, but it overlooks the social and economic circumstances within which the parable was first crafted. So with that introduction, let's enter, as best we can, into the world of this parable that has been renamed by a recent parable scholar as 'The Vulnerability of the Whistleblower', I'll try to unravel meaning in the parable, drawing heavily on the interpretation offered by William Herzog. while inviting you to draw what parallels and challenges to our day occur to you.

In the time of Jesus, Galilee was in a process of significant social change. The older village economies were breaking down as the area became more and more embedded in the economic system of the Roman Empire. Whereas families had traditionally owned and farmed their land, this communal style of living and sharing was breaking down. The introduction of the plough (replacing the hoe) and the domestication of animals had led to greater agricultural production and the development of trade with other parts of the Empire. An emerging elite class, whose lavish lifestyles contrasted with the essentially simple lives of village dwellers, accumulated surplus wealth. This elite class purchased and sold the produce of farmers, making considerable profits from trade deals with other parts of the Empire and collecting taxes on behalf of the Empire.

The ancestral land of an increasing number of families fell into the laps of this elite class when they were unable to repay high interest on loans to enable the purchase of seed or other necessities. Ancestral land offered as collateral was lost and former landowners were reduced to being day labourers seeking what work they could during harvest time. The saying that 'the rich get richer and the poor get poorer' was certainly true of first century Galilee. Jesus saw it as a demonic system in urgent need of change.

Along with these changes came the rise of cities modelled on Greek cities in other parts of the Empire. In these cosmopolitan centres, Roman customs and values dominated life and the ancient wisdom of the Hebrew tradition was drastically modified or set aside. These emerging cities formed an extensive economic and political network that between them controlled the surrounding land and villages. Wealthy elites, shaped by Greek customs and dependant on Roman support, had strong links with the military and the religious leadership was largely in their pocket and did their bidding. They controlled society. The bulk of wealth and influence was in the hands of perhaps 2% of the population who controlled most of the wealth of the society. A group of about 5% who served the needs of the elites were well rewarded for their efforts while the rest – peasants, artisans, the unclean and the 'expendables' – lived simple and insecure lives. This was the 'Kingdom of Rome' or the 'world-system' that Jesus contrasted with his very different 'Kingdom of God'. Our parable, like other parables, is a parable of the 'Kingdom of God' so prepare yourself for a counter-cultural surprise!

The Kingdom of Rome in Galilee prospered because there were sufficient locals who were willing to dedicate their lives to the continuing prosperity of the elite class – in return, of course, for a generous share of the power and prosperity that belonged to their masters. This really got up the noses of the ordinary folk. People they knew, members of their extended families with ability, turned their backs on their own people and threw in their lot with those who oppressed the ordinary people of Galilee. These functionaries who served the policies of the elites were paid a modest salary but this was easily supplemented by extra financial demands they could add to the burden already carried by the poor. Members of this bureaucracy, those serving the commercial and political ambitions of the wealthy elite, were kept busy – overseeing agricultural production, ensuring that the olive, fig, dates and grape harvests were successfully harvested, employing day labourers to assist the harvest, collecting taxes on behalf of the Empire and interest on loans was paid on time.

Commercial ventures like the fish-salting factory in Sepphoris near to Nazareth needed to be carefully managed if targets were to be met and production was to be sufficient to meet the needs of the larger Empire. Fishermen had to be urged to work hard so they might repay a loan for the purchase of their boat or nets or to meet production goals laid down by their masters. No part of Galilean society was free from the tentacles of the 'system' or the additional charges that lined the pockets of those who worked for the elites. The whole society was caught in a net that served the needs of the wealthy at the expense of the poor and of the traditions that had previously shaped life. Jesus had strong opinions about these matters and he sought change. Don't buy into the convenient lie that Jesus was not concerned about politics or economics!

Our parable envisages a situation when a man of wealth left the bureaucrats in charge while he was absent on a journey. Perhaps he was travelling to inspect his estates in other parts of Palestine or perhaps to other parts of the Empire in search of new markets for Galilean produce or perhaps in search of promotion within the power structures of the Empire. The staff who are to care for the estates during his absence are described in the parable as 'slaves' but the term 'retainers' or 'bureaucrats' might be more appropriate. They are ranked according to their place in the staff pecking order. Out translation states that each of the workers is given a sum of money 'according to his ability'. A better translation suggests that they were each given an amount 'according to their power', i.e. their rank or status. Roman society was status conscious in a way that contrasted sharply with the more egalitarian village societies that Jesus sought to perpetuate.

A 'talent' was a measure of weight and in this context represents considerable wealth. During the master's absence, two of the staff members knew exactly what to do with the money entrusted to them. They made more and then more. Ancient law prescribed the minimum annual profit an owner could expect for himself was 100%. The two bureaucrats successfully deliver this generous return while not disclosing what they have earned for themselves. The only source of profit for themselves is lending money to peasant farmers and fishermen at exorbitant interest rates and taking possession of land or boats when the loans could not be repaid. They will have earned their profit, for themselves and for their master, off the backs of the poor – from their own people. Like many before and since they knew how to work the system to their advantage! They've been co-opted into the system and their consciences have been totally dulled. Their minds and spirits have been colonised by the system. They're happy to receive their reward. It's legal but is it moral?

The third retainer is the focus of the parable and bears the deeper message within the narrative. He's an interesting and courageous fellow. He's prudent inasmuch as he returns the original amount to the owner. But, more importantly, he refuses to be co-opted by the system that serves the comfort of his master and could serve his comfort too but which damages the lives of workers. He simply refuses to play the master's game! Instead he attacks the master as an exploiter who benefits from the hard work of others while enjoying a luxurious life style for himself and his family. In refusing to sell his soul to a system that enslaves others, this 'third man' exposes the unjust nature of an economic and social system that serves the privilege of the few at the expense of the many. The third servant is vilified, shamed and humiliated – that's the price to be paid if you won't play according to the rules of the game devised by those with power.

Our third servant is a 'whistle-blower' who names injustice that others have regarded as normal and been willing to go along with. His action is reminiscent of the way Moses left a life of luxury and privilege in the palace of the Pharaoh and identified with the plight of his enslaved Israelite people. He stands in the tradition of the great prophets like Amos, Micah, Isaiah and Jeremiah who criticised those 'who trample on the needy and bring ruin to the poor of the land' and who called upon the nation to seek justice above all else. In telling the truth and acting upon a deeper wisdom than that available in the house of the aristocrat and among his mates, the third servant, the whistle-blower, declares the possibility of another way of organising society – one shaped by honesty, generosity justice and a care for the needy. His action becomes a sign of the presence of the life-affirming Kingdom of God doing battle with the pervasive and life-denying Kingdom of Rome and its successors right into our time.

I think of pacifists who refused to serve a system claiming to make peace through violence, of people living simply rather than worshipping greed-based capitalism, of people refusing to live within expected race based prejudice. It's common that those who refuse to march to the tune played by the dominant system are punished for their refusal to play the approved game. So we are told the whistle-blower is thrown into 'outer darkness'. In the darkness of social deprivation, he'll doubtless find a sense of community and support with others whose lives have also been damaged by the actions of those who, though wealthy in money terms, are really paupers of the spirit.

There seem to be parallels with our day. Are we too ruled over by spiritual paupers whose only god is money? Are we among them? There's plenty to ponder in this parable.

Jesus is portrayed in the Gospels as a whistle-blower supreme. Don't buy into the convenient lie that Jesus was unconcerned about politics! His dream of what could be and his courage in naming defects in the imprisoning systems of his day made him far more political than the everyday politicians of his day. I suspect this parable would have encouraged early Christians to emulate the actions of the third man – to simply yet profoundly refuse to cooperate with economic, political and social systems that promote death rather than life. Some at the time suggested violent insurrection to change society. The third man in our parable, like Jesus in his ministry, chose non-violent resistance. Is he a utopian fool or is he a courageous man embodying the way of Jesus?

How do we as individuals and corporately as a church contribute to justice and peace and the building of a society freed from greed-based economics, unjust treatment of fellow citizens and peace-denying attitudes? It's a continuing challenge to those who follow the Jesus-way and reach out toward God-Kingdom. The pathway is not simple and our strength as a Christian community is not great. I have no simple solutions to offer but the question hovers around in parables like this. Should we keep silent, say our prayers, swallow our convictions and, like the first two men in our parable, serve our own comfort from within a system we know to be unjust? Or, are there non-violent ways of refusing to serve systems that deny food and shelter to the poor, support to refugees and promote damage to the environment? Which character in the parable best describes the church, as we know it – the two compromisers or the troublesome third man? What do you think?

Exploring Further

William Herzog's parable book is well titled: *Parables as Subversive Speech, Jesus as Pedagogue of the Oppressed* (1994). More than any other parable scholar I know of, Herzog places the parables into the context of the first century experience of oppression under the colonising rule of the Roman Empire. He demonstrates how we have domesticated the parables by our description of them as 'earthly stories with heavenly meanings'. They are like illustrations in a handbook on how to live within God-love in a time of serious oppression by a ruthless system. Another helpful and recent parable book is: Amy-Jill Levine (A Jewish scholar teaching in a Protestant seminary), *Short stories by Jesus – the enigmatic parables of a controversial rabbi* (2014).

3

A moment of grace for the prodigal family
Luke 15:11-32

> I first preached this sermon in a large South Korean church in an abbreviated form and helped by a translator. The discussion that followed was lively, especially as the women identified with Mrs Prodigal and her hidden role in the parable. In preparing this sermon, I clearly placed contemporary observation of life ahead of commentary-based wisdom.

The parables of Jesus are little tales with a sting in the telling; and whose definitive meaning can never be pinned down. They come alive with fresh insight and challenge when entered into with a simple desire to live within the way of life pioneered by Jesus. Today, I want to re-enter the Parable of the Prodigal Son, offering a sort of alternative, yet everyday, interpretation of these well-known words. Like many of the Gospel parables, it tells of how the grace and mercy of God are hidden in the folds of everyday life.

The story is about a family. The family is not named so it could be any family. It could be our family, our church, our

A moment of grace for the prodigal family Luke 15:11-32

neighbourhood. The story was first told in first-century Palestine but the dynamics within the family have a universal feel about them. There are four characters in the parable.

The first we could call Mr Prodigal senior. Like any first-century father, he's well aware of the responsibilities that fall on his broad shoulders. He's hard working and liked. His friends know he's anxious about his family's future. He carries disappointments about his sons, especially the younger one who, he feels, is headstrong and rebellious.

This younger Mr Prodigal is an impatient fellow. Home has become uninteresting and dull. He wants life and he wants it now. He wants to try out life in the big world. His parents sometimes wonder if they were not strict enough on their younger son.

The older Mr Prodigal, the elder son, was brought up more strictly than his younger brother. He's a great worker, disciplined and dutiful. His parents wonder if he'll ever leave home and create a family of his own. He's comfortable and contented with mum's cooking and seems bolted to the floor of the family home. Father Prodigal has noticed with deep pain how critical this hard-working and dutiful son is of his younger brother. Sibling rivalry is a tough issue even for the wisest parents.

The fourth character in the parable is not named or mentioned. She is the mother of the boys and the wife of Mr Prodigal senior. She remains silent like all wives were at that time. But she was there. She felt the pain of her husband's disappointments and she cried when she thought of how her two boys failed to be good friends. She was familiar with near sleepless nights, sometimes blaming herself for the family failings.

The family might have stumbled along for a long time, not particularly happy but getting on with what needed to be done. Mrs Prodigal worked behind the scenes to keep the three men in her life on speaking terms with each other. Then came the big day! It was at the dinner table after a hard day of work. The youngest son announced to his parents and brother: 'I'm sick and tired of life in this family. I feel stifled. I'm tired of working for you father... work, work, work... I need some time to play'. Then he turned to his brother: 'And I'm tired of living in your shadow Mr Goody Good'.

He asked for a share of the inheritance that would be his when his father died. He received it without so much as a thankyou and stormed out of the house. It would have been one of those tense family occasions that are best not to dwell on. One of those times when things are said that cannot be taken back and which fester and keep you awake at night.

Perhaps the lad was half right. There does come a time when children need to leave their parents and strike out on their own. It can be hard for parents to let go and leaving children are often not above offering harsh and hurtful criticism of their parents as they leave. But in claiming his inheritance, treating his father as though he were dead, the boy would have really hurt his parents who, for all their shortcomings, were not short on love. No parents are perfect but they do their best.

In the weeks and months following this dreadful occasion, the Prodigal family would have felt restless and angry. The parents wondered were they'd gone wrong in the way they'd cared for their second boy. Parents have an enormous capacity to blame themselves for the shortcomings of their children. It's as well Mrs Prodigal was not aware of her son's adventures in a distant land. Even without knowledge, her worries were vivid and debilitating. In fact, things didn't go well for the lad. He fell in with a bad crowd and his money melted away like water being swallowed by parched ground.

Then came the day when the younger boy returned to his home. The parable tells of how the son prepared what he would say to his parents. No doubt his parents had often discussed how they would act and what they'd say if by chance that scoundrel of a son, that spendthrift, who had bought shame and dishonour to his family should return.

We know from Sunday school days what happened. The father's welcome to his son was extravagant. He welcomed him as though he were royalty. The family ring was placed on his finger and he was clothed in the best that money could buy. To the surprise of the neighbours, the father threw a party for the son who had wasted his father's money and had brought such deep pain to his mother. He was invited to banquet with friends and family, to a place of hospitality, of forgiveness and new beginnings.

The elder son grumbled when he saw these things and complained to his father: 'Hey, what about me? I might be dull but I have never given you a sleepless night. Look at my hands and see how I've laboured hard and long in your fields'. The father replied, 'My son, put aside your anger and your jealousy. All I have is yours, come and enjoy the feast. Come to the banquet, the place of hospitality, of forgiveness, and new beginnings'. His words were the same to each of the boys: 'Come to the feast, there you will know you are loved and valued'.

This is the central moment in the parable. The words and actions of the father represent what we might call a moment of grace. Grace is like light shining in darkness and showing a way into newness; it's a sense of possibility crowding out despair. A moment of grace comes to us like a gift of water in a dry desert. Grace is a sense of new beginning gifted by God through the actions of others. To be graced is to know in the depths of our being that we are loved, valued, trusted and needed. Grace is most commonly experienced in community so in the parable it's represented by a banquet. Because grace is a gift of God, we cannot create it or distribute it as though we own it. But we play a crucial role in creating the conditions under which grace can run free and let loose its transforming energy. Christians are people who, like the father in our parable, are learning how to intervene in life in such a way that space may be created so that grace may happen – in families, in workplaces, in neighbourhoods, where there's conflict, where life is stuck for any one of a thousand reasons.

The older Mr Prodigal let go of anger and imagined a new future for his boys and their family. He apparently appreciated the struggles going on in each of the lads. He moved beyond a win-lose scenario and created a situation where everyone might be renewed. Future possibility rather than past errors became his focus. He stopped talking for long enough for silence to allow fresh thinking, new awareness of what could be to surface in the lives of each member of the family. The human family desperately needs people who create the space wherein grace might operate and take wings. We need people like Mr Prodigal senior who sense possibilities for healing rather than retribution, forgiveness rather than punishment, hospitality rather than alienation, truthful relationships rather than self-righteous one upmanship. We need people like Mr Prodigal senior who, acting with love, restraint and a gentle honesty, create spaces in life where the healing grace of God may break through and bring newness to birth.

We don't know if the youngest Mr Prodigal turned his life around or if the two brothers were reconciled. What we can know is that these things were more likely to happen in the atmosphere of acceptance, forgiveness, honesty and generosity that the father had created. Some people seem to be born with the knack of creating openings for grace to flow. For others, the learning of this gentle yet vital art comes more slowly. Participation in the community of Christ and meditation on how Jesus opened the gates of grace and allowed the renewing love of God to flow freely are traditional and enduring ways through which we learn how to create occasions when the grace of God may flow freely.

Perhaps this is a primary element in what it means to be a Christian presence in the communities where we live – creators of those moments when the grace of God is set free to work miracles of renewal, forgiveness and newness in a wounded and divided world.

Exploring Further

There's no shortage of books, chapters and articles on this well-known parable. The best of them link the three parables about lostness in Luke 15. A farmer loses a sheep, a woman loses a coin and parents lose a son. In each case, the parable ends on a note of celebration – don't let who and what is most important be lost. Perhaps their lostness adds to their value, their importance to the community. An excellent exposition is in Amy-Jill Levine, *Short Stories by Jesus* (2014). As in all parable interpretation, it's important not to turn a parable intended to provoke us to an imaginative exploration of life into an allegory where every question is answered and every character and action stands for another person or action. Is the father in our parable standing in for God, or is he any father struggling with the meaning of fatherhood and an erring child? Does the elder son stand for those who rejected Jesus in the first century or does he stand for every child struggling with sibling rivalry? And the erring son?

4

The rich man and Lazarus
Luke 16:19-31

> The challenge implicit in the parables of Jesus continues through history. Sometimes, it seems they were first spoken into our time and place – ancient words that continue to challenge and inform later times. Gospel parables are like literary hand grenades thrown into the placid pool of everyday living and exploding with a disarming capacity to question what we take for granted along with an invitation to explore new ways of living in the name and spirit of Christ.

Today's Gospel parable of the Rich Man and Lazarus is about freedom, bondage and what it means to share in God's healing purposes for humanity. I have no doubt the rich man in our parable believed he was serving the purposes of God and contributing to the healing of the world by his loyalty to the social and economic assumptions of the privileged class into which he had been born. In fact, he had overly identified himself with a 'system' that brought suffering to many in first-century Palestine.

The parable has two scenes. In the first, the setting in first century Palestine is obvious. It was a socially and economically

The rich man and Lazarus Luke 16:19-31

divided society. Economic injustice was rife and social discrimination was commonplace, the result of economic changes introduced by Roman overlords who, with the support of a small but powerful Jewish political elite, were turning Israel into a source of fish, oil and other products for their Imperial masters. They were desperate days for the poor, who made up the bulk of the indigenous society.

The two characters in our parable represent the extremes of a socially and economically divided society. The rich man is an urban elite who dresses in imported luxury and takes it for granted that he was born for such privilege. He has no obligations to the poor for, after all, he might claim, life is a level playing field and everyone has the opportunity to make it to the 'top'. He would have assumed his privileged position was a gift of God. Lazarus, the destitute beggar, lives on the edges of society, perpetually hungry, and because of ulcerated sores probably shunned as unclean. He competes with the dogs of the street for the left overs from the table of the rich man – a sort of first century version of the trickle down economic theory used to justify the wealth of the privileged in our day.

There would have been no surprises for first-century readers of Luke's Gospel. This was the way society was. Only those who read and pondered the ancient scriptures where a new society shaped by sharing, hospitality and care for the needy was imagined would have questioned the status quo. These hopes of a new society were kept alive among the poor, who, because of the sufferings of the present, hoped for a future when God's love would penetrate the nation's life. The wealthy, like our rich man, rarely hope for a new future, for change for them could only mean loss of privilege. In ignoring the plight of Lazarus and even building a great gate to keep such wretches at a safe distance, he was simply following the unexamined assumptions of the class into which he had been born.

In scene two, we leave the harsh realities of first century Palestine and enter the heavenly courts. This section of the parable is not a treatise on the geography of the afterlife, rather an imaginative way of having a peek into the mind and purposes of

God, a sort of look behind the scenes to catch the meaning of what's happening. The rich man is horrified to learn that he's got it all wrong. He has not been serving the healing purposes of God as he assumed. Rather, he has been destroying life by self-centred living. The poor had few weapons to defend themselves against the power of the wealthy in first century Palestine but humour was among them. There were many stories told in the Middle East at that time about wealthy citizens who found that after death they were shut out of the pleasures of God's companionship while their underprivileged workers were rewarded.

Our parable is a Christianised version of one of these tales. It would have been told to keep hope alive among the poor while also enabling them a laugh at the expense of the powerful. I recall Bishop Tutu, at a conference I attended in Kenya in 1986, using humour in the same way. He said that, while the Apartheid-loving white regime in South Africa felt secure in their privilege, God looked down and laughed at their pretensions. The future, he said, belongs to the little ones, and God will bring this new reality to birth. He invited us to laugh at oppressors everywhere for their reign will come to an end. So the pretensions of the powerful are cut down to size by the holy laughter of the poor.

The relevance of this ancient parable to us who live more than two thousand years after it was first crafted will, I hope, already be apparent. Its meaning is certainly not exhausted by its first-century application. There is an implicit theology in the parable that is worth exploring further.

The setting of the parable is the human tendency to divide, denigrate and ignore those who do not belong to our particular social or economic grouping. Locked into the privileged social class into which he was born, the rich man cannot see the needs of Lazarus. He is blinded by his own social privilege. He suffered from an illness that is still damaging the lives of many – addiction to affluence. Among all the addictions to which humans are subject, this is probably the most damaging and powerful. In the

The rich man and Lazarus Luke 16:19-31

search for ever-increasing wealth, those addicted to affluence can never get enough money – their house is always too small, their power is always in search of expansion. Families, neighbours and particularly the poor and vulnerable pay the price of their dreadful and damaging affliction. Healing for this rich man is simple but demanding – to take down the shutters that blind him to the impact of his addiction on others and to reach out to them as friend and colleague in the journey of life.

We were all born to live together in community. Differences of culture, wealth and power will always exist but none of them is sufficient to justify our ignoring the higher call to friendship in the presence of difference. Had the rich man used his undoubted social power to dismantle the walls that divided rich from poor, clean from unclean, privileged from destitute, ruled from rulers, he would have become an active participant in the healing work of God.

Each year in the Uniting Church in Australia in New South Wales, congregations were invited to participate in a 'Great Sunday of Sharing' and to visit a congregation that represented different cultural, social and economic values than their own. While serving in the working class and Tongan-dominated Parish of Auburn in Western Sydney, we developed a link with Killara, a wealthy northern suburbs parish. Our folk prepared well for our first visit into this 'alien' territory. They wondered if they would be well received in such an up market area. We took over a hundred folk, a great heap of Tongan food and apprehensive hearts. It was a great day. Our choir filled the leafy neighbourhood of Killara with the sounds of the Hallelujah chorus and, after the service, traditional Tongan food was eagerly devoured while the conversations between 'them' and 'us' went on and on. On the way home, our folk expressed surprise that the good people of Killara asked how they could get some of the sense of community and enjoyment of life that was as natural as breathing for our Pacific bunch. We all need experiences where barriers are broken down and understanding and appreciation is allowed to flourish.

In our parable, the poor man is named while the rich fellow is nameless – he was parked on the 'no names' shelf of life. There was nothing special about him – he was simply playing a role in life. He read from a script prepared by others and slavishly followed it. He was a slave to the sort of behaviour that went with his privileged place in society – just a cog in a larger money machine. Lazarus was poor but he was a 'somebody'. A name, given by our family and used by our friends, is a badge of belonging. It's a sign of our God-given uniqueness. The first step for the rich man in escaping from his social conditioning might begin with him learning how to address others by name and also inviting them to use his personal name.

The end of the parable includes the puzzling refusal of God to allow the rich man's family to be warned of their mistaken understanding of life. The reason is simple – change of this sort is human work. Those who have a privileged position in society need to take the first steps on the road to understanding and sharing community. Only when they give up talking of the poor and needy as suffering from some sort of self-inflicted ailment and step out of their comfortable clubs and start to build creative relationships with those for whom life is tough, will the revolution of healing compassion be released in our societies.

The church fulfils its God-given task as we allow ourselves to live in a larger and more generous world than the narrow world of privilege into which we might have been born or perhaps have achieved by education or good fortune. One of the challenging things about the Christian way is learning to be self-critical about our own involvement in the perpetuation of injustice and division in our world. In terms of the parable, we might see our larger task as being to dismantle gates that keep Lazarus from joining us at the table of life and that perhaps lock us away from authentic participation in the healing of God's world.

The rich man and Lazarus Luke 16:19-31

Exploring Further

A good book on the parables and their first-century origin is Bernard Brandon Scott, *Hear then the parable: a commentary on the Parables of Jesus*, (1989). If the first step in understanding a parable is to enquire into its probable original meaning, the vital second step is to allow ourself to be questioned by what we read – to allow the parable to live again, to move from printed word to lived life.

5

Human greed and a world suffering the effects
Luke 19:1-10, Matthew 6:24

> It's not possible to follow the Jesus Way and remain unaffected by the crisis brought on us by climate change and environmental destruction. We soon find ourselves questioning taken for granted values that underlie our western way of life.

Our service this morning began with a hymn reminding us the environmental threat that faces humanity and which imperils the future of human civilisation as we have known and enjoyed it. ('At the dawn of your creation' by Carolyn Wilfrey Gillette, tune: Hymn to Joy.) The sad truth is that this alarming environmental degradation has resulted from long standing foolish and selfish human behaviour.

The readings are about the perils of wealth. Jesus' suggestion that one cannot serve both God and money can be paralleled in the words of other great religious leaders and founders. They are words we know well. They are part of the essential furniture of the Christian way.

Human greed and a world suffering the effects Luke 19:1-10, Matthew 6:24

The story of Zacchaeus is equally well-known within the Christian community. A man so deeply addicted to affluence that he is willing to work for the Roman machine and, in its name, to fleece his own already struggling neighbours while he adds to his already considerable wealth. He glimpses another possibility for life in the way being pioneered by Jesus and gets rid of what he now senses is destroying himself and his community.

We return to the hints within our opening hymn: as a human race, we are in a mess. Readily available and widely published research into the effects of climate change and environmental degradation paint a bleak and frightening picture of the future that awaits us. Every day brings fresh reports of damaging heat, droughts, floods, extreme weather patterns, rising sea levels, species destruction, the retreat of glaciers ... and much more. If rising sea levels continue as predicted, many of the great coastal cities of our world will be flooded, today's horticultural areas will become desert-like. Climate refugees moving around the world in search of water will become commonplace.

I could go on enumerating facts you know but have learned to live with. Like me, you too might mentally turn off when the TV news brings yet more ghastly evidence of the mess we are in - it is all quite depressing, even more so when we are reminded that human action encouraged by an economic system actively promoting the plunder of nature has brought us to this dire position. Even if we were to dramatically reduce our polluting behaviours, the effects of centuries of such behaviours would cause civilisation-damaging changes. This is the future our grandchildren will inherit and inhabit.

As individuals and societies, the story of Zacchaeus could be our story. Can we, like Zacchaeus, escape from our 'addiction to affluence' or what someone described as 'growth fetish'? The question could be rephrased: could we, like Zacchaeus, learn to share so that the vast, community-damaging and growing economic and social gap between the rich and the poor might be lessened, so that everyone might have sufficient money and resources to live a decent life? The questions seem so huge that it is perhaps understandable that we sidestep or ignore them. However, for us the words and wisdom of Jesus linger: 'You cannot serve God and money'.

In some sermons, preachers present a problem and set out by the conclusion to offer a solution that can be acted upon. That is certainly not the case today. I simply raise a question, seeking answers that require more than twenty minutes of an individual's inadequate words. It requires continuing discussion within the church community as we explore the Zacchaeus possibility and, in the wider community, as we draw on ancient wisdom to address important contemporary issues. Incidentally, the story of Zacchaeus is preceded in Luke by a story of a rich ruler (Luke 18:18-25) who was so attached to his wealth that he was unable to embark on the Jesus way of living. It is a realistic story, one still enacted in our day and which makes the Zacchaeus story all the more amazing. Together, these two stories again offer their own commentary on the ancient wisdom, 'You cannot serve God and Money'.

The Gospels contain a great deal of discussion initiated by Jesus about the perils of possessions. The Gospel of Luke is particularly concerned about the hazards of wealth. It is sometimes said that Luke has more to say about money than prayer; not because prayer is unimportant but because wealth has such a power to divert us into destructive ways of living. Money has a strange power to possess people, take over their lives, pervert their relationships, and engage in violence and even warfare against those who have what they want. Greed-based accumulation of money is a powerful drug – more powerful than the illicit drugs that rightly worry us and cause us to fear for the safety of our young ones.

In the time of Jesus, Palestinian village life and its values of sharing, generosity and forgiveness, were under threat from the greed-based economy promoted by the Roman military and

Human greed and a world suffering the effects Luke 19:1-10, Matthew 6:24

political presence. It's easy to spiritualise the words and deeds of Jesus but a fair reading of the Gospels presents him as leader of a village-based movement promoting both spiritual and social renewal. Jesus clearly stood within the values of the village rather than those represented by the Roman presence. In one memorable parable he suggested workers should be paid according to their need rather than the hours they worked. In another, he described a man unable to build sufficient barns to house his wealth but unexpectedly died without ever truly living life. He gained the world as defined by his greed but lost his life as defined by his relationships. The teaching of Jesus is similar to that of the Buddha who defined human greed as the cause of suffering and as the human trait most in need of radical change.

John Wesley, 18th century reformer, social activist and theologian, preached often on the spiritual and social dangers caused by wealth. In a notable sermon on 'The use of money', he suggested that we should earn all we can by honest means, save all we can and, most notably, give away all we can. He died a poor man, having followed his own advice but not long before his death complained that too many members of the Methodist movement he initiated had grown wealthy and had lost their love for the way of Jesus. Wesley was certain that the goal of life is to grow in love, contributing to the well being of our neighbour. Greed, addiction to wealth, is a hindrance and a deep and persistent human problem. Both capitalist and communist economic systems demonstrate the same problem. Though each claims to promote human well-being, neither has learned how to share wealth so that no one remains outside the circle of those who have food, shelter, friends and worthwhile work. Both encourage human greed as a primary driver of the economy. Both are addicted to growth in the economy even though the price paid by workers and the environment is overwhelmingly high.

Human greed plus access to fossil fuels has brought us to the dreadful situation we now find ourselves in. Even when aware of the effects of our greed on the world of nature and the future awaiting our progeny, we, as a human race, struggle to break away from our addiction. The development of money was a significant event in human evolution and it brought many benefits. However, no longer was surplus food shared with neighbours. Instead, everything had a price sticker placed on it and the prices soon came to reflect corporate greed rather than intrinsic value. There is so much more to be said but my task is simply to point us all once again to the ancient wisdom that 'you cannot serve God and money'. We know what money is. Let God be understood as the deepest love and best possibilities for human living and environmental well-being. You cannot serve the deepest good and the best possibilities for human living and at the same time be a servant of money.

It is strange that, given the extensive references to money in the teaching of Jesus, it is so little spoken of in church life. I recall as a young minister, smiling in amusement as each year, on Stewardship Sunday, the church treasurer rose and apologised that he had to speak of money! Perhaps there should be more rather than less discussion about money and its power over us in normal church life. It is encouraging that in many Christian denominations, accumulated capital is now being invested in social housing and programs to benefit the poor. One church has appointed a task group to develop a theology of wealth and property. It is good news. However, their preliminary material for discussion placed much emphasis on the church's wealth being 'a gift of God'. Gift language may have merit if it indicates something not earned and therefore to be shared but 'gift of God' language is dangerous when applied to accumulated wealth. It's more likely to be the result of fortunate stock market fluctuations and property prices rather than gifted by an approving deity. I hope they make a clear statement to the church that the so called 'prosperity gospel' (the claim that those who follow Jesus will be rewarded by expanding wealth) is a dangerous heresy and should be condemned as an undermining of the gospel. Perhaps they will recognise that a 'user pays' way of funding parishes has failed.

Parishes in the most socially needy parts of society have been closed because they cannot meet the costs of parson, property and all the other costs that go with being a 'main line' parish. Perhaps some of the accumulated wealth of the church can be invested in the most needy parts of our society (the poor for whom Jesus had a special care), developing new ways of being a Christ-influenced presence in partnership with medical, educational and other people-helping agencies. The early church, according to Acts 4:32ff, sought to keep alive the village values promoted by Jesus, sharing wealth and building supportive community. But as the church spread into the cities of the Roman Empire the attractions of wealth and the ways of Roman imperialism took over. Even the Franciscans, an order founded to perpetuate the witness of St Francis the poor man of Assisi, grew in wealth and settled down within the system.

As we work with others seeking to build a just and environmentally sustainable society and world, we will need to draw on our deepest and most honest wisdom. The story that the meaning of life is to be found in the accumulation of money needs to be exposed as a lie. It is a significant part of the ancient yet living wisdom for which we, as people of the Jesus way, are responsible.

Exploring Further

A church report was published, called '*A theology of money and property*'. Though encouraging wealthy parishes to share their wealth with financially poorer parishes (within the provisions of church property law), it failed to grapple with deeper questions of how idolatrous love of money has perverted the gospel, destroyed the environment and damaged human community. Those wanting to explore the issues further will be helped by Daniel Bell, *The Economy of Desire – Christianity and Capitalism in a post modern world*, (2012) and Scott W. Gustafson, *At the altar of Wall Street – the rituals, myths, theologies, sacraments, and mission of the religion known as the Modern Global Economy*, (2015).

6

Neighbours!
Luke 10:25-37

> Yet again I'm dependant on the insights of a biblical scholar who has helped our generation to enter afresh into a biblical text we thought we understood. I like the way that in the scholarly world, hard working researchers share their wisdom.

The Parable of the Good Samarian is probably the most preached on or the most referred to passage in the New Testament. As a generalisation, you could say we've sussed out the meaning of this example story – whether we're good at it or not, we know what we could, might or should do in the presence of another's need. We're to act like the Good Samaritan.

But it's dangerous ever to assume we've arrived at the definitive meaning of a parable. Parables come alive in fresh ways as they're read in new circumstances and within a fresh willingness to be questioned by what we read. The meaning and questions a parable brings to us often depends on whom we identify with in the parable. So, in this parable, we've been taught to identify with the good guy – the generous and caring Samaritan. We may not be as good and caring as he was but we know we've got it in us to act in the same way. It's courage we need if we're to follow the Samaritan's good example.

Today, I want to retell the story and invite us to identify with a different character. First a little background from the workshop of biblical scholarship. There's a near consensus that the parables belong to the original words of the historical Jesus. If you want to get into the essential message of Jesus, the parables are a good place to start the journey. The tricky bit is determining which parts of a parable represent the words or sentiments of Jesus and which words were added by the Gospel writer in an attempt to give the parable a believable context within the writer's particular telling of the Jesus story. Scholarly detective work suggests that in this parable the introductory question of the lawyer about how we might inherit eternal life is a later attempt by Luke to give a context to the parable that follows. Similarly, the final words from verse 36 asking which of the three potential helpers in the parable was a true neighbour to the unfortunate victim feels like an attempt by Luke to impose his single interpretation onto the parable.

Many years ago, I came across an alternative reading of the parable by Robert Funk, who limited the probable words of Jesus to verses 29 to 35 and suggested, correctly I think, how this parable might be reinterpreted for our day and probably how Jesus intended it to be interpreted. ('The Good Samaritan as Metaphor', *Semeia 2*, 1974)

I'll tell the parable and invite you to play your part in it. 'A man went down from Jerusalem to Jericho.' The man is un-named. He could be any Jewish person. You be the man on the journey from the harsh desert surrounding Jerusalem to the green and lush area surrounding Jericho. It's a difficult journey through a deserted area where thieves often hid in caves. Normally, people travelled in groups for protection but you're silly enough to travel alone. Sure enough, robbers strip you, beat you and leave you half dead in a ditch by the roadside. Without your clothes, you're stripped of all that might indicate your social class. You're just another

Neighbours! Luke 10:25-37

anonymous victim in a dangerous and sometimes violent society. The first hearers of our parable would recognise the well-known Jericho road and the dangers that might accompany a journey to Jericho. You who set out on the journey with high hopes are now lying in a roadside ditch, in great need and annoyed at your misfortune. Funk suggested that a suitable title for the parable might be 'The view from the ditch'.

'By chance a priest passes down the road.' Perhaps he's on his way to the Temple to fulfil his priestly duties. To your dismay, the priest sees you in the ditch but hurries by. Does he think you're dead and that he'd make himself unfit for Temple service if he touched a dead body? Or is he just another hypocritical clergyman, all talk and no do, more interested in privilege than service? Priests who first heard the parable would cry 'foul' and 'cheap shot' but there was enough anticlerical sentiment among the common folk for this unexpected turn in the tale to be greeted with laughter.

Then 'a Levite also passes by'. The question is being rammed home: Do even the best among us put status ahead of the ancient command to go to the aid of a neighbour in need? From your place in the ditch and in spite of your injuries, you can barely suppress your mirth at this twofold kick aimed at the guardians of religious conformity.

In parables, things usually happen in threes. Surely now a Jewish layman will come to your aid. The anticlerical suggestion will be rammed home. No hearer expects the next move in the tale: 'A Samaritan who was travelling came near and was moved with pity'. A Samaritan! You can tell by his clothing he's a Samaritan and you're afraid as he comes near. Since childhood, you – like all Jewish children at that time – were taught to distrust Samaritans. They had once failed the nation at a time of need and were regarded as traitors and heretics. Diligent Jews even avoided passing through Samaritan territory lest they be religiously polluted. In spite of your anti-Samaritan prejudices you're in great need and you accept the stranger's compassionate care. The impossible happens. This unnamed Samaritan enemy of Israel goes the proverbial second mile and takes you to an inn and covers the cost of your care. Your tidy world of 'good Jews' and 'bad Samaritans' is shattered.

Robert Funk concludes his reading of the parable: 'in the Kingdom of God, mercy is always a surprise'. It comes from unexpected quarters. If a distrusted Samaritan can be an agent of divine and healing compassion, then any group can similarly be an agent of God's healing purposes. Goodness is not the sole possession of one group or of those who follow our way. When we identify with the Samaritan hero in the parable and see ourselves as being Samaritan-like in our generosity towards those in need, we're subtly claiming our place among the strong entrusted with a divine mission to be servants of humanity in a way that no one else shares. When we identify with the man in the ditch, we're acknowledging we too are needy. The challenge becomes: are we willing to receive help, mercy and healing wisdom from those we've been taught to distrust, even hate with a religiously inspired hatred.

Recently, I read an account of how a church had created and maintained an orphanage for needy children. It's a great story of Samaritan-like service by a host of good people. But nowhere is it suggested that the church might also receive a gift from these children. The children are described as statistics, helpless beneficiaries of the kindness of others. The author never asks what we might learn from the coping mechanisms developed by those children. Did these children have intuitive wisdom from which others might learn important and potentially life-giving insight? Or don't 'Good Samaritans' need to learn from those they help?

We tend to read parables in a way that will confirm our goodness and place in the sun. Identified with the man in the ditch, we're invited to recognise that for all our sophistication we too can be among the needy and uncertain in society. And furthermore we may need the wisdom, the compassion and the friendship of people we've been carefully taught to distrust. On talk-back radio recently, I heard a woman describe her sense of surprise at being helped by a bunch of gang members when her car broke down in a lonely place. Like distrusted first-century Samaritans, they overcame her fears, fixed the car and set her off on her way. In the Kingdom, mercy comes from unexpected quarters.

A few years ago, I accompanied a troubled mother to Sydney to follow the trail of university failure, gambled money, broken friendships and fear left by her son over a two-year period she believed was a period of study. After a day following this dreary and painful litany of failure and waste, it was time for the mother to receive effective support from caring people. I'm not without church connections or friends in Sydney but I chose to take her to a Muslim school and cultural centre. She was welcomed with warmth, invited to share time with the children and in the evening invited to share beautiful food with caring and newfound friends. She had been taught since childhood to distrust Muslims. In the Kingdom, mercy comes from unexpected quarters.

There's a human tendency to create little enclaves of security where we can feel good about ourselves and from where we can look over high walls at the poor, mistaken and needy wretches who live outside. We may help those outside our zone of safety but we rarely accept help from them. But, what if, in the mood of the parable, we were to acknowledge we're all to some extent viewing life from within a ditch and we need the wisdom, the hospitality, the discoveries, the compassion of other people regardless of where they're from and what label they carry? The parable viewed from within the ditch invites us into a world where barriers of prejudice are being melted away by an awareness that we're all together in life and it's foolish to divide the human family up into goodies and baddies, acceptable and unacceptable, Samaritans and Jews, good Christians and pagan others. Perhaps we need to get out of the tribal 'ditches' where we hide from those who are different – and it doesn't matter who helps us out. Come to think of it, the whole world's in a ditch of enormous need, prejudice and violence. Collectively, we need all the wisdom, compassion and courage we can muster, regardless of where it comes from, to get us back on track on our journey through the wilderness and to the lush and green pastures of Jericho.

Exploring Further

Amy Jill Levine warns Christian interpreters not to fall into an old trap of painting the priest and Levite as symbolic representatives of an outmoded, out of touch, and unloving Jewish way that is contrasted with a new way of compassion represented by a Christianised Samaritan. It's the sort of shoddy scholarship that has fed Christian caricatures of Judaism, helping to feed prejudices that led to such a distrust of Jewish people that even Hitler's holocaust was justified by German churches. Jesus was a Jew who sought the renewal of the tradition he had been brought up in and continued to value. Amy-Jill Levine, *The Misunderstood Jew – The church and the scandal of the Jewish Jesus* (2006), is a good way into an important discussion.

7

Good Samaritan? You've got to be kidding!
Luke 10:25-37; John 4:3-26

> Preachers who follow the three year ecumenical lectionary know that meanings that were clearly grasped three years ago may surrender a different punch line three years later. The biblical text has not changed but the questions and concerns we bring to the text, the matters troubling us and our society, will have changed. Like a conversation with an old friend, old words take on new significance in new circumstances. I'm comfortable with the interpretation of the Good Samaritan printed above but, in 2022, I preached on the same text and it came out differently. It could as easily have become a sermon based on the story of Jesus and the Samaritan woman (John 4) but on this occasion, the old parable became our doorway into an important dimension of Christian ministry.

It must surely be a good thing that today four churches in Napier City, committed to working together for the common good, should each be reflecting on what it might mean to live in this city in the spirit of the parable of the Good Samaritan.

We all know the parable. Its uncomplicated invitation to be compassionate toward any neighbour in need is inescapable. We care for neighbours in need because every person matters; every person is a child of God. Each of us has had times, or will sometime, when we need the care of compassionate neighbours. We are all inter-connected and love is the golden web that holds us all together. The parable is at once an invitation to care for the needy and marginalised and a dream of a world where no one is left alone on the roadsides of life without a hand to hold in times of need, good food to eat, a house to live in, the assurance that, though tough times may come, yet we will not be left to struggle alone. Perhaps the parable is also a reminder to us that true religion is not so much a matter of loyalty to creeds, rituals and churchy systems but a way of living shaped by compassion, generosity, simplicity and care for others.

I want to explore with you another dimension of the parable that also needs to be heard in our day. As I walked around these well-known words again, I imagined the sort of discussion that might have followed among Galilean villagers attracted to the Way being explored by Jesus and who had heard this wee tale for the first time. I would have liked to be a fly on the wall as they discussed and perhaps argued about what Jesus had said that day. They needed no reminder from him that they were to care for strangers and aliens. But many perhaps most of the first hearers of this parable would have been offended that it was a 'Samaritan' that is praised as being a good neighbour.

For villagers in first century Galilee, 'good' and 'Samaritan' simply did not belong together. First century Jews were taught from childhood years that Samaritans were not to be trusted, believed or taken seriously. Their wisdom was ignored and rejected. They had no secure social standing in Galilean villages. They kept to themselves. People didn't argue about this judgment -

Good Samaritan? You've got to be kidding! Luke 10:25-37; John 4:3-26

it was simply one of those taken for granted and unquestioned assumptions that was accepted without further discussion. So those first hearers might have debated whether, if they were robbed and left wounded on the lonely Jericho road, they would or should accept help from a dirty Samaritan (those you've been taught to hate are always thought of as dirty and unattractive). I can hear the words of some: 'I'd rather be dead than have the hands of a Samaritan touch me'. Few of them would have met a Samaritan or talked with a Samaritan, yet they were united in their distrust of Samaritans. Even without meeting a Samaritan, first-century Galileans just knew they were bad news.

Every culture, every national group, seems to be home to a cluster of unexamined prejudices, attitudes and behaviours that are passed on from generation to generation. In Galilee, the story was told and retold of how centuries earlier the ancestors of the Samaritans had failed the nation of Israel in an hour of need. They had cooperated with the national enemies and had even married Assyrian soldiers. Stories were told in Galilean homes, schools and synagogues of how the Samaritans had betrayed the faith by building altars to foreign gods and welcomed those who followed pagan ways.

It was recalled that when Jewish leaders exiled to Babylon 500 years before the time of Jesus were permitted to return to Israel, the Samaritans refused to welcome them back and to assist in the rebuilding of Jerusalem. Instead, they built a rival temple on Mount Gerizim. Samaritans were regarded as being 'unclean' and because of an assumed link between people and land, the area known as Samaria (today the West Bank) was also regarded as being unclean. It was the custom at that time that no loyal son or daughter of Moses should pass through Samaria on a journey to Jerusalem. Rather, pilgrims going to Jerusalem for the great festivals should walk around rather than through Samaria.

In spite of this commonly held prejudice against Samaritans, Jesus spoke positively of them. He is portrayed in the Gospels challenging what he apparently regarded as an irrational and ungodly prejudice against Samaritan neighbours. When Jesus and his disciples, on their way to Jerusalem, passed through Samaria and were not received by the locals (Luke 9:51-56), Jesus refused to endorse the anger of the disciples directed towards these inhospitable Samaritans.

Another story describes Jesus healing ten lepers but only one, a Samaritan, returned to thank him. Then there's the extraordinary story of Jesus' encounter with a Samaritan woman at a well (John 4:1-42). Their conversation includes discussion of the woman's personal circumstances, relations between Samaritans and Jews, relations between men and women and theological disagreements that divided their two communities. Jesus is portrayed taking this Samaritan woman seriously – respecting her views, listening to her life story and engaging with her in serious discussion. As a first century woman and as a Samaritan, it would have been a new experience to be taken this seriously by a Galilean Jew.

According to these stories, Jesus simply refused to buy into the well-worn and socially accepted prejudices against Samaritans. Jesus was inaugurating a new way of being human and of building society. Whereas most ask who is to be excluded from our community, who doesn't really belong, Jesus asked, who is not being taken seriously, whose wisdom and experience is not being heard? Jesus' question was not who should be excluded but how can we include those who are not being heard? Samaritans seem to have been remembered by those who later wrote the Gospels as a sort of test case of Jesus' attitude to those on the margins, those they had been taught to distrust. The parable of a caring Samaritan, a man who overturned all the inherited prejudices against his people, was treasured as a parable of the new world Jesus was bringing into being – sometimes called the Kingdom of God.

He was a boundary breaker – he welcomed all manner of people to share his meals, to discuss with him what they hoped for, how they could cooperate in the building of a more gentle, more just, more peace-loving society. Slowly, it dawned on those who first reflected on what Jesus had taught them – he was inviting them to unlearn all the nonsense they had been taught about enemies and allies, us and them, winners and losers, servants and masters, rich and poor and instead to imagine and work for a society where every person, every group, each with their own experience and wisdom, was taken seriously as bearers of God-spirit and given a secure place in an inclusive and caring society.

On a day when we ask, 'Who is my neighbour and what does it mean to be a neighbour in the spirit of Jesus?', we might also ask 'Who are the "Samaritans" in our society – who have we been taught to distrust, who are denied the possibility of contributing their wisdom to the building of our shared society, what prejudices directed against this or that group in society do we need to unlearn? How can we, in the spirit of Jesus, open doors to enable their full participation in our society?'

It seems to me that Jesus, as portrayed in the Gospels, not only cared for the needy, he enabled them to speak for themselves, to claim and cherish their own God-enveloped wisdom. The Samaritan woman Jesus conversed with remained a woman rather than a feminine body with a male mind. She remained a Samaritan rather than a scaled-down Galilean. Jesus enabled her to speak as a Samaritan woman, to be proud of who she was and to claim her place in his emerging society, placing her wisdom, insight and experience alongside what others brought to the building of the new society Jesus was putting together.

I can think of many groups in our society who qualify to be thought of as metaphorical 'Samaritans' – people whose humanity is denied, whose wisdom is disregarded, who are ignored by the powerful. Think of refugees and migrants. Think of Maori who even in their own land and with their positive role in society guaranteed by a treaty, were for more than a century listened to only if they thought and spoke like brown-skinned settlers. In our day, there is an exciting renaissance of Maori perspectives. They are contributing to our emerging society from within distinctively Maori wisdom and experience.

Or think of the Muslim community in New Zealand, until recently distrusted and feared lest they bring violence to our shores. Fear and distrust of Islam has been part of the very air that too many Pakeha, including Christians who should have known better, breathed and passed on to their children. As a former Co-President of the NZ Council of Christians and Muslims and from my close relationships with Muslim communities in Sydney and Auckland, I have felt their pain. And then came 15 March 2019 and the murder of 51 praying Christchurch Muslims. We all felt their pain, their humanity, their vulnerability to hatred hatched from within the white supremacist community.

Last year, St Columba's Church, Havelock North, hosted Farid Achmed, a wheelchair-bound Muslim leader, whose wife was among those murdered in the Al Noor Mosque on that fateful day. We listened spellbound as he spoke of forgiveness and of how every person is a child of God. His words were profound yet simple. He shared wisdom born from within the Muslim community and magnified by deep grief. We were all indebted to someone many had previously thought was a member of an alien, 'Samaritan-like', culture. The truth is that we're all together in the single bundle of life and we need each other's wisdom, energy and experience if we're going to make it through the challenging decades ahead. We need to let go of prejudices that divide. We need to learn to listen, to respect and to include every group, every person, every neighbour – every one of them a child of God. Every metaphorical 'Samaritan' is to be welcomed, respected and given a voice.

I said I would have liked to listen to hear how 1st century Galilean villagers responded to Jesus' outrageous story of the Parable of the Good Samaritan. I'd be even more interested to listen to a discussion among the members of the four Napier congregations who today are reflecting on the same little story from long ago. I wonder what new ways of being present in this society are emerging?

Exploring Further

I made only a brief reference to how Maori and other indigenous peoples have historically been treated in a 'Samaritan-like', marginalised manner in western societies. An inexpensive little book, *Imagining Decolonisation* (2021), by a group of Maori academics and activists, elaborates helpfully on the brief mention I make in the sermon. Its relevance extends beyond New Zealand. Incidentally, you may like to consider how Christian faith and churches have been 'colonised' by capitalist greed, nationalistic ambitions, a search for power over other ways, a place in the sun denied to others. Are we too in need of decolonisation? Have we – like indigenous pathways – been taken over, our deepest wisdom ignored, captive to non-gospel ways of thinking, feeling and living?

8

Good seed, poor soils and God-grace

Genesis 25:19-34; Matthew 13:1-9, 18-23

> Many of the parables draw on rural practices so it's not surprisingthat Jesus became known as a sower of seeds of life and of possibility. But it's not a simple exercise, then or now. We're all seed sowers but what sort of seeds?

Today's readings invite us to think about the mystery and form of God's presence within the human adventure. The suggestion is that God plays on a larger canvas than can be embraced by our neat systems and sharp-edged judgments as to who is right and who is wrong, who lives within God's purposes for humanity and who are outsiders. As I felt my way into the story of Esau and Isaac and into the parable of the sower, I found that the two readings each threw light on the other.

The Genesis reading continues the tale of the somewhat dysfunctional family of Abraham and Sarah. They may be celebrated

Good seed, poor soils and God-grace Genesis 25:19-34; Matthew 13:1-9, 18-23

as founding figures within Jewish, Christian and Muslim communities, but the story is a somewhat sordid tale of a family shaped by violence, jealousy, fear, bigotry, greed and manipulation. We're asked to believe that this dysfunctional, fragile and limping family is the vehicle through which God's presence within the human adventure was enacted. We're asked to believe that, in spite of their appalling behaviour, they are people whose sensitivity to God's purposes is an example we might learn from.

The stories surrounding this family were passed on and eventually written down and included in the holy books because those who read them saw themselves – both their frailties and their possibilities – in the adventures of Abraham and Sarah, Hagar and Ishmael, Isaac and Rebekah, Esau and Jacob. They treasured these stories as examples of how God could use human frailty, weakness and wrongness, in the search for communities shaped by peace, justice and hospitality and of how even fragile people like these could be responsive to the presence and leading of God. The Abraham saga is a sort of good news story: God uses human weakness as well as human strength in the fulfilment of creation's promise. There's room for all of us, weak and strong, foolish and wise, the certain and the uncertain, those full of faith and those of limping faith. If God chose Abraham's foolish lot to lead the revolution, then there's room for us all within the Divine purposes.

The parable of the sower suggests that the energy we call God is forever sowing seeds of possibility in every human life and inviting those who are willing to be agents of the way of life pioneered by Jesus. God is understood in the Gospels as a gracious love that reaches into human living, empowering ordinary people and assuring them that their living is of significance in the unfolding of evolution's promise. God is portrayed as being like a wind that blows through life, a love that cannot be controlled by temples or dogmas, systems or moralities.

The parable of the sower is included in each of the synoptic Gospels as a pictorial summary of the ways people responded or failed to respond to Jesus' declaration of new possibilities for human living. We're invited to imagine Jesus as being like a sower throwing out seeds of possibility in a generous and wasteful manner. He's portrayed in each of the Gospels as a somewhat free-wheeling preacher whose life is like an acted parable of divine love, searching for a future that knows no boundaries and embraces everyone regardless of their social, economic or political status.

His ultimate rejection and crucifixion comes about because the seeds he sowed fell on some pretty barren land. Some, like the disciples, welcomed his invitation to share in the work of blessing the world, a task begun by Abraham and expanded by Jesus. But when the going got tough they deserted for their commitment to newness was hesitant and incomplete. Others were so locked into the values that belonged to the privileges they enjoyed that attempts at following the Jesus way were soon snuffed out by their captivity to social, political and economic systems from which they could not free themselves. Others seem to have grown spiritually deaf and were unable to fully appreciate or understand the possibilities he offered. They were, according to the parable, like barren or unfertilised soil.

What of those described as being good soil within which the gospel seeds could grow and bear fruit? According to the larger gospel story, it was the poor, the marginalised, the sick and the erring who responded to the invitation to join Jesus in the search for a new society and new ways of being human. Because they experienced the present as a time of personal and communal pain, they were open to the Jesus dream of a society shaped by hospitality, justice, generosity, forgiveness and peace. Those who lived in tidy boxes, those shaped by rigid and judgmental morality and those locked into rigid theologies watched as seeds of possibility withered on the parched land that defined their insensitivity to anything that promised newness. There's a similarity between the family of Abraham who, within their weakness, were nonetheless sensitive to the whisper of God's call and the similarly unsophisticated and bruised bunch that made up the first followers of Jesus.

Good seed, poor soils and God-grace Genesis 25:19-34; Matthew 13:1-9, 18-23

As the church developed and grew in power, the parable of the sower was re-interpreted. The church, led by popes and parsons, rulers and rogues, the wealthy and the wily, claimed the right to define who was good soil and who, in their judgment, was a barren and unproductive dump of dirt. People of the good soil, it was claimed, were those who accepted the teaching of mother church, who believed what they were told to believe, who were virtuous and who served the comfort of those who claimed to have been chosen by God to rule, to prosper and to play God. The barren soil was defined as the place where heretics, the disenfranchised poor, rebels against injustice and those who refused to kill in the service of their masters were to be found. Jews, Muslims, Buddhists, Hindus and Sikhs, Chinese, Turks, Africans and Polynesians, it was believed, all lived on barren soil and wandered through life apart from the support of the God of Abraham and of Jesus.

That's the official story. Fortunately, there was another tradition, represented by mystics and rebels, dissenters and the marginalised, who kept alive the story and experience of God's love present in every human life and particularly among those on the margins of society. For a large part of Christian history, the church in all its forms has acted as a harsh and judgmental presence in life. There's often been little room, even tolerance, for those who might have belonged within Abraham's dysfunctional family. The sad irony is that the church, self-appointed guardian of the gospel, became a prime example of hard soil existence, resistant to the explosive energy of God and captured by forms of life that served its own purposes and comfort. We're privileged to live in a time when it's becoming widely recognised that those of other faiths and of none may be living on good soil and may have internalised attitudes we had thought belonged only 'our' Jesus and 'our' church.

The distinction within the parable between good and barren soils should not be regarded as final statement about any person or group. Each of us is, without doubt, a mixture of soils. We all have our blind spots. We're all on the way, learning how to receive the way of Jesus into our living. Yet our partial following of the way of

Jesus is enough to make a difference in life. If God could use the dysfunctional family of Abraham and the poor and marginalised of Palestine to serve humanity, to be reminders of the goodness of life within the love of God and the possibility of the human family being healed, then we too may have a role to play in the healing of the world.

The church is wise to live with humility, aware that God paints on a larger canvas than the one painted by the church. The good soil is present among people far removed from the institutional church. I'm sure many of us have been surprised by signs of the Christ presence in the lives of people and organisations we had have assumed lived on unresponsive, gospel-denying soil. God paints on a large and inclusive canvas. The overall image of the sower is a fruitful one for the church in our day. As individuals and as a community, it's our privilege – in spite of our obvious weaknesses and deficiencies – to throw our gifts and whatever wisdom we have into the pool of life, trusting that God can and will use what we do, what we pray and what we say, in the healing of the world. We sow with humility for we don't know everything and there are limits to our energy and strength. If the family of Abraham could contribute to the healing of the world, then perhaps we too can make a difference.

Exploring Further

Have a look at the church budget and identify expenditure items devoted to maintenance of what is and those that are expressions of seed-sowing, exploring possibilities, risking what we have in service of what might be. Seed-sowing is a chancy business as all gardeners know – the weather might be too dry, too wet, the wind too fierce, the slugs too hungry. But just keep sowing.

9

Good news, bad news
Matthew 20:1-16

> Some say that, though history doesn't repeat itself, it does rhyme. Here's another parable that rhymes with possibilities and questions relevant to our times.

The village-based renewal movement of Jesus was good news to those who suffered under the imperial rule of Rome but for those who benefitted – socially, politically and economically – from the Roman presence, the same message and actions were received as bad news to be opposed at all costs. Good news to the poor tends to be recognised as bad news by the well-heeled and socially advantaged.

Today's parable is a good news/bad news story. It's typical of the parable form that while some hearers are comforted, surprised by unexpected grace, others find themselves to be challenged and questioned, identified as hindrances rather than healers of life. Parables are good news to some but bad news to others. Their purpose is not to give us new information but to jolt us into new ways of thinking and acting. They question us; they flush us out from the secure places where we hide from the purposes of God and the kingdom of grace. The meaning of the parables of Jesus is never exhausted. They are like music that echoes down the corridors of human history, speaking in fresh ways to every generation, provoking, questioning, unsettling, as ancient wisdom interacts with the challenges and possibilities of new days. They are discussion starters – invitations to newness.

The story line of the parable of the compassionate landowner was simple and recognisable to first-century Galilean hearers. They were times of economic and social change, and consequently of religious uncertainty. The old, well-tried patterns of village life were breaking down as the Roman Empire extended its grip on every area of Galilean life. Galilee had become a source of cheap food – fish, olives, grapes and wheat – to sustain the life of a rapacious army and a building program designed to celebrate Imperial achievements. Heavy taxes led to debts unable to be repaid and the loss of small peasant holdings to a newly emerging class of urban-based large landholders. The relatively simple social and economic structures of village life were being destroyed by heavy taxes and the luxurious life-style of an emerging entrepreneurial class. Our parable reflects the first century situation of too many Galilean peasants. Those who once farmed their own modest bit of land were reduced to sitting around in the village square in the hope they might get some day work and be able to feed their family. There was high unemployment in first-century Palestine.

The workers in our parable accept the offer of the landowner because they have no bargaining power – they work without a clearly stated contract and accept the risk of working for less than what they deserve. The householder holds all the economic trump cards in his dealings with otherwise unemployed peasant workers. The custom of engaging workers for only a day at a time ensured that workers remained in a weak bargaining position. Shaped by economic and social circumstances like this, Galilee was like a powder keg that could erupt at any time. There had been rebellions against those who benefitted from the Roman occupation but none had succeeded.

Our parable, like other parables, brings together representatives from the extremes of Galilean society – on one hand a landowner who benefits from the new economic structures and on the other peasants who are reduced to picking up scraps of income that fall from the tables of the wealthy. Commentators suggest that the payment of a denarius a day was not a generous wage but was probably sufficient to enable a family to live at a subsistence level.

An important clue to the interpretation of a parable is to identify the point of surprise in the narrative, the point where expectations are overturned and we find ourselves to be questioned and invited to reconsider what we have hitherto taken for granted as being reasonable, moral and normal. The surprise in the parable of the compassionate landowner comes in verse 10. The manager, on behalf of the landowner, pays the same to each worker regardless of hours worked. It's preposterous, economic lunacy, socially disruptive behaviour, and an offence against a rational and sustainable economic system.

I can imagine the response of the first hearers. Some within the peasant audience would cheer, others might smile and whisper to their neighbour: 'if only!!' Others would laugh for humour is one of the great ways of keeping hope alive in tough times. Others, like the long-term workers in the parable, might have commented on how offensive it was for everyone to receive the same. Others would be saddened at the attitudes of the complaining workers who had so internalised the views of their masters they had lost the ability to rejoice at the good fortune gifted to the most needy of their number. The term 'dole bludger' was, as far as I know, not current in biblical times but there was probably an equivalent and it would have got a good workout among the first hearers. Perhaps others sensed an invitation to join in social and economic disobedience and to a revolution that would put an end to injustices imposed by the greed of Roman imperialism. Any landowners in the crowd would have felt confirmed in their judgment that Jesus was a hopeless but dangerous fool who must be stopped.

The central figure in the parable is the landowner. It was simply not believable that a beneficiary of Roman privilege would act in this way. He was clearly a traitor to his class and to the system that benefitted him and his friends. Generosity like his would soon undermine the system that his privileged position was built upon. In every age, those who enjoy privilege usually regard the systems that maintain their wealth as being 'normal'. Those who challenge those systems are regarded as unstable, irrational, disruptive, crazy and unpatriotic.

His extravagant actions serve to draw attention to the injustice and exploitation that was embedded in the economic and social structures of the time. The alternative to what he did was to pay those who were employed later in the day less than they needed to feed their families and so assign them to the impoverished margins of society. The landowner's actions highlight the essential injustice and exploitation of the poor that lay at the heart of the nation's economic life. It was coming to be accepted that not every worker would receive a living wage and that a successful economy required a pool of unemployed peasants. Apparently, the landowner was suggesting there is a living income below which no family in first century Israel should fall. Good news for the poor, bad news for the bosses and their bottom line!

It would have taken courage to challenge the system in the way done by this imaginary landowner. It's still a difficult thing to do. Few people have the courage to challenge economic, political and social systems that damage their neighbour. Even fewer have the courage to challenge systems that serve their own comfort while assigning others to a difficult life. The parable, in its first-century setting, is suggesting that change in that increasingly unjust society will only come when the well-off give up their privileged position, learn generosity, work for a just society and place the needs of the poor ahead of their own extravagant comfort. The landowner claims his freedom to buck the system and to act for humane values that cry out to be expressed. He frees himself from the power of a system that he now recognises is unjust to his neighbour. He's apparently been converted to a new way and is trying to work out the consequences in practical terms. The parable raises some interesting questions about first-century Palestinian society but what about today?

Theologically, the parable affirms the centrality of grace in human living. I don't mean grace as a chapter in a theology textbook: I mean grace as a way of life lived in response to God - love. Grace is generosity beyond calculation; it's a valuing of hospitality over judgment; communal justice over individual wealth. It emerges from a deep-down conviction that God's love is extravagant, universal and generous and that authentic human living is our being shaped by this love lived out amid the ambiguities of human living. It is a happening. It is a gift.

It's unlikely that we'll take the actions of the landowner as a literal blueprint for twenty-first century economic restructuring. Yet we shouldn't forget there are Christian communities where everything is shared, no one receives more than another and no one has less than they require to live. Such extreme gospel living keeps important gospel questions alive. We need so-called extremists like this for they remind us of dimensions of life and of the gospel we might otherwise lose. We need pacifists who, in a world ready to go to war at the behest of ambitious politicians, remind us there's another way. We need teetotallers who remind us there are social consequences of alcoholic consumption that need to be factored into decision-making.

The suggestion that initiative for change and the promotion of a just society lies with the well off who feel the pain of the poor and disadvantaged is a continuing challenge for Christians in denominations that enjoy the advantages of affluence and social privilege. Most of us who hear and meditate on this parable will continue to live within economic and social systems that benefit us and others like us – but as long as we remain within the Christian community there will be a restlessness within, questions that will not go away, questions that linger. The question might be posed: can we claim the courage and freedom to question instances of injustice, racism, sexism or violence that, though embedded in our society and taken for granted, damage the lives of our neighbours? How can we live out the implications of grace in a somewhat grace starved society? Can we, like the landowner who broke the rules and provided a space where grace might grow, create fresh signs of a more caring society? Can we complete the parable; live out a conclusion to it for our time and place?

Exploring Further

The parable, like others in the Gospels, raises sensitive questions about the injustice woven into the economic system that shapes our life together. Those who study the Gospels will soon find themselves wondering about how we, as a human family, can reshape the ways we distribute wealth, care for each other, care for the environment. A recent book by Philip Clayton and Wm Andrew Schwartz, *What is Ecological Civilisation* (2019) will take you into this crucial debate. Another is David C. Korten, *Change the Story, Change the Future – a living economy for a living earth* (2015). Our crisis time, brought on by climate change and the gap between rich and poor, is sharpening the thinking and imagining of many.

10

Fishing nets, God-love and a needy world

Matthew 4:12-23

> The old chorus, 'I will make you fishers of men...' always troubled me. Even as a teenager, it sounded arrogant and potentially manipulative, as though we are on a fishing expedition, looking for scalps in some great religious competition.

The story of how four fishermen were invited to follow Jesus and to use their gifts to fish for people has played a large part in defining the nature of Christian living. It seems to me that the words, 'Follow me and I will make you fish for people' have made both a positive and a negative contribution to the church's understanding of its life and mission. I'll begin with reference to the social and economic background within which these words were spoken, then develop the view that in popular Christianity the image of being 'fishers of people' has been seriously misused and has distorted the presentation of Christian faith. Then in an attempt to salvage the image of net fishing I'll draw on a Buddhist myth in the hope it might assist us as we continue to puzzle over the nature of Christian living and how that way might be commended to others

Jesus' choice of four fishermen to be among those who would support and encourage him in his life work is significant, for these hard-working men had no social, financial or religious status. This was to be a movement built on the contribution of those from beyond the accepted economic, religious and political power blocs that dominated that society. Matthew makes it clear that the Jesus movement for national, social and spiritual renewal was to be a people's movement rather than a political program devised and imposed by the powerful.

Fishing played an important part in the economy of first-century Palestine and many tradespeople – net makers, boat builders, fish processors, those transporting fish products to a nearby port – depended on this industry and the physical strength of those who fished. Initially a family activity, catching sufficient fish to meet the daily needs of an extended family or perhaps a village, it had become a large state-controlled industry serving the demand for dried or salted fish, pickled fish and fish oil for export to other parts of the Roman Empire. What had previously been a seasonal occupation conducted by lakeside families between the sowing and harvesting periods had, by the time of Jesus, become an industry generating great wealth for some but modest reward for those who did the hard work.

Roman officials had oversight of the industry and sold fishing rights to brokers who in turn contracted the right to fish to locals. Loans to enable purchase of boat, nets and other equipment ensured that fishermen remained indebted to the brokers who in the Gospels are referred to as tax gatherers or publicans. An agreed portion of the catch went to the brokers who in turn contributed to local Roman officials. It was a system that was resented in the villages of Galilee.

In inviting the four to turn their backs on their trade, Jesus was inviting them to leave an occupation that though providing enough to feed the family also locked them into an insecure and exploitative Imperial economic system designed to serve the already wealthy. While the invitation to follow him seems to come out of the blue, we can assume the fishermen would have known of the convictions that shaped Jesus because of his public identification with the renewal movement promoted by John the Baptiser.

Jesus invited the four to serve the Kingdom of Heaven or Realm of God rather than the Empire of Rome. (Matthew speaks of the Kingdom of Heaven rather than the Kingdom of God out of respect for the Jewish reluctance to use the name God.) For him, speaking in the tradition of the prophets, it was an either/or choice God – Kingdom or Roman – Kingdom. The four fishermen were invited to join Jesus in exploring what it might mean to serve the purposes of God rather than the purposes of the Emperor. In leaving behind what they knew, Peter and Andrew, James and John were embarking on a risky journey into an unknown future. To follow Jesus remains into our day as a simple yet deeply profound and demanding way of describing what it means to be Christian. However intellectually sophisticated we may have become, we live from the simple affirmation that we follow Jesus, working out the changing implications of that choice as life unfolds. There are no certainties and the meaning of our following unfolds as we proceed on life's journey.

What of the suggestion that the four will become 'fishers of people'? I've found no commentary that gives a half decent explanation as to what these words might have meant when originally spoken or if not actually spoken by Jesus, what they meant to the Gospel writers. Perhaps it's a poetic suggestion that the tough qualities needed to fish in Galilean waters are the same qualities needed by those who set out to live for the rule of God in a time dominated by the rule of Rome. Or does it mean that in the future they'll be part of a movement embracing people who, like them, come from the margins of society?

What is clear is that the words, 'you will become fishers of people' have had a powerful and not altogether helpful impact on the church's understanding of its life and mission. In later centuries, Protestant evangelists and missionaries claimed it as a primary image by which they might understand their task. Evangelism came to be understood as being like a fishing expedition, catching people one by one and adding them to the basket of the captured. The church's primary work was understood to be saving people who, uncaught, might perish in the sinful seas of the world and who would certainly suffer beyond death in a place reserved for those who failed to acknowledge Jesus as their saviour. Such a view generated an urgency to capture those whose eternal destiny depended on our fishing skills but it also encouraged somewhat aggressive and manipulative behaviours.

It's a view that remains popular in our time. I looked up 'fishers of people' on Google and came up with references to some amazing organisations building on this image. One showed a large fishing hook and invited readers to share in baiting the hook so that fish might be saved from the fires of hell. Over the years a two-stage baiting of the hook was developed: first, convince hearers they were sinful, hopeless, deficient and fit only for punishment. Then, when they felt sufficiently guilty, assure them that Jesus had accepted the punishment due to them and had opened the doorway to heaven.

Sadly, this caricature of the Christian way, this dreadful misappropriation of the image of first-century fisherman-disciples, invited to think of themselves as gatherers of people rather than catchers of fish, is believed by many beyond the church to represent mainstream and authentic Christianity. It's among the difficulties liberal-progressive Christians face. The title 'Christian' has become identified in the minds of many with attitudes and beliefs that pervert the essential message of grace at the heart of the Christian way. The division of people into the saved and the unsaved, the fishers and the fished, those on their way to hell and those with a secure place in heaven, of a God who will punish those who refuse to take the bait, represents a dreadful caricature and perversion of the way pioneered by Jesus.

The appalling judgmentalism that accompanies such ways of thinking and acting is a denial of what it means to follow Jesus. It's not clear how the Christian way can gain a fair hearing in today's western society but rejection of the image of ourselves as fishing for people with all the paternalistic and manipulative overtones it has gathered over the centuries is an important first step.

Pondering these things and still attracted to images associated with nets, fishing and the following of Jesus, I was reminded of the Buddhist metaphor of Indra's net. In the heavenly home of the great Indian god Indra. there is, according to ancient tradition, a wonderful world-embracing net. It is home for an array of beautiful jewels woven into the net in such a way that the beauty of surrounding jewels is reflected in each of these precious and irreplaceable stones. Mahayana Buddhists see in this image a reminder of how life is made up of relationships, of how all of life is a unity. While each jewel is beautiful in its own right, its true beauty can only be seen in its relationship to others held within the same net. In Christian terms. we might say we are held within the net of God's love and our true life is found as we live in relation to other people who are also exploring what it means to live within that love. Our destiny and fulfilment is in learning to live together as members of a single interconnected world.

We belong within God and we belong to each other. Evangelism is not a matter of catching individuals with a carefully baited hook and rescuing them from a sin-infected and hell-bent world. It's an invitation to follow the way pioneered by Jesus and to contribute to the patient task of working towards a society and a world where everyone's place within the life-enhancing love of God is acknowledged and defended. In a divided and frequently violent and unjust world, it's good news that, in spite of human foolishness and divisive behaviour, we live within the net of God's love and we each have a role to play in ensuring that no one is left out from the net of human compassion.

The good news we offer is that the human family is a single body held within a net of love. We fulfil the church's evangelistic ('good newsing') task as we welcome others to join us in exploring what it means to live within the net of God – love. It means to live for unity and compassion in a world where each person is recognised as a jewel of ultimate value and where society is becoming a human embodiment of Indra's net. Inasmuch as we pursue this path we are responding to the invitation of Jesus, 'Follow me'.

Exploring Further

> Leo Lefebure, *Life Transformed* (1989), is a series of beautiful reflections on the words of Jesus in the light of Buddhist perspectives. The gospel we thought we knew and understood takes on an enriched meaning in conversation with the wisdom of other faith perspectives.

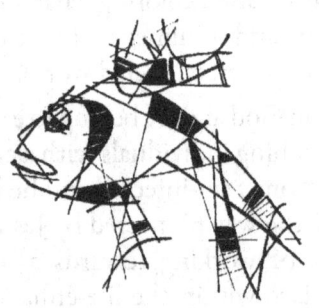

PROTECT THE WALL OR PLANT THE SEEDS?

The Western church's problems are more than declining numbers and waning influence in an increasingly secularised culture. The deeper problems have to do with a collective lack of imagination, a waning sense of adventure and, deeper still, a reluctance to explore afresh the Way pioneered by Jesus and to ponder what form that Way might take in our creaking world. The church is still home to some wonderful people, many of whom bear the scars of a long journey in their search for all that the Way of Jesus represents in a wounded world. Like Jacob who, in the ancient story, wrestled both with God and with his own possibilities, they walk with a holy limp (Genesis 32:22-32). Sometimes, important aspects of the Jesus Way seem more alive among those who, though no longer part of organised religion, seem to embody qualities previously identified as Jesus qualities.

In congregations of traditional denominations, aging members recall more energetic days when church programs were vibrant and life-giving. Though weak in energy, they remain strong in hard won wisdom. They wonder what form Christian mission might take in the absence of energy but the presence of wisdom. Numbers are down and it is often a struggle to maintain and finance church plants and denominational structures designed for more buoyant days. A decades-long struggle to maintain a semblance of unity while engaged in sometimes fierce denominational debate on a variety of important social and spiritual/theological issues has diminished energy, exacerbated existing divisions and lowered confidence. Attempts by migrant groups to maintain understandings of Christianity presented to their people by nineteenth-century missionaries has created a zone of security for their people but has often made it difficult for younger members to fully participate in the fresh exploration of the Jesus Way our times demand.

Pentecostal and Fundamentalist versions of church have expanded in recent decades. They vary greatly but many draw inspiration from the Bible belt of the USA and, like them, have chosen to identify with far right politics, the rejection of scientific research into the nature of evolving reality, religiously sanctioned conservative social attitudes and a harsh rejection of wisdom valued by religions and cultures other than their own. They have energy but often lack wisdom. Embrace of the 'prosperity gospel' – the strange view that those who acknowledge the importance of Jesus will be rewarded with monetary wealth – reflects a dangerous view of God. Their well-known lack of respect for the LGBTI community is a puzzling stance for people claiming to live within the compassionate way of Jesus. If they were to move beyond the aridity of fundamentalist ideology and to explore the Way of Jesus in a broader and more world affirming and inclusive manner their energy and enthusiasm could become a positive contribution to the healing of a wounded world.

The Salvation Army operates from within a conservative theology but maintains a commitment to the needs of the poor and needy that has become part of the national ethos. Along with the social service agencies of other denominations they contribute to the maintenance of a caring society. The Society of Friends, or Quakers, though small in number, maintains a focus on peacemaking that keeps alive this vital dimension of Christian living.

The Church of Rome remains intact as an institution conscious of its long history and worldwide influence but appears theologically and spiritually divided and humiliated by damaging scandal. Its universality and the leadership of a sensitive and thoughtful Pope are genuine strengths as is the remarkable leadership offered by women scholars and sisters of teaching and serving orders.

Every part of the Western Church is in need of renewal. But what sort of renewal? Surely not a reinforcement of creedal obedience or programs to grow bigger, brighter and wealthier congregations and denominations. Authentic renewal must surely begin with a fresh and compassionate facing of our needy world along with a sensitive and thoughtful re-exploration of the way pioneered by Jesus. Who knows what organisational shape will emerge for the emerging church? Life comes before structure. At least that's what Jesus thought as he imagined the renewal of the Faith into which he had been born: 'No one puts new wine into old wineskins; otherwise the wine will burst the skins, and the wine is lost, and so are the skins; but one puts new wine into fresh wineskins' (Mark 2:22).

I am reminded of a parable of a farmer and his wonderful pumpkin. He grew the best pumpkins in the county and each year won the prize for the largest and most beautiful pumpkin. This year, he lovingly tended a most beautiful pumpkin he planned to enter in the annual competition. But alas, one day, he visited his pumpkin patch to find that his prized pumpkin was collapsing. Its walls were literally falling down; its golden flesh was turning to mush. His first instinct was to prop up the collapsing walls, to perpetuate its life sufficiently to show it in the county fair. Days went by and the walls continued to fall, the once beautiful pumpkin became misshapen. It was collapsing. It was then that he saw that he could no longer prop up the collapsing walls of a pumpkin he had so loved and that had brought him great joy. Better, he decided, to let it collapse and instead gather seeds still alive within its flesh, plant them, let new shoots flourish, new pumpkin possibilities be born.

1

Rediscovering the adventure

Mark 1:1-14

> There's an unfortunate assumption that only the youthful are attracted to adventure. My experience is that. in all but the most extreme circumstances. there's room for another adventure, another risk, another step on the Way.

The writer of Mark's Gospel was convinced that in Jesus' life, something of enduring importance for human living had been enacted. He wrote his Gospel a short time after the fall of the Jerusalem Temple, during the Jewish revolt against Roman oppression. Without the Temple, focus of Jewish religious and social life and popularly believed to be the dwelling place of God, many – including Jewish followers of the Jesus way – wondered if faith could survive the loss of such a life-shaping institution. Mark wrote to assure members of house churches in Northern Syria that the purposes of God were not, and would never be, defeated by the destruction of human structures no matter how important they seemed to be. His strongly held conviction is that Jesus represented and will continue to symbolise the presence of God in human life.

As I pondered our Gospel reading and sought a point of entry for a sermon on Jesus and John and their meeting at the Jordan, my attention was grabbed by three images or allusions through which Mark describes, hints at, the significance of Jesus. They seem to be as relevant today as when first written.

When Mark's first readers or hearers heard the first words of the Gospel: 'The beginning of the good news of Jesus Christ' they would have instinctively recalled the first words of the Hebrew Bible: 'In the beginning God created...' The suggestion is that Jesus represents a new creation, a fresh explosion of God's creative love for humanity. Many 21st century Christians consider that the life and teaching of Jesus represents an evolutionary possibility for human living, an expression of new ways of being human. I certainly do. Mark knew nothing of evolution but evolutionary thinking is compatible with his suggestion that Jesus represents a new creation or an important event within the continuing work of creation in an incomplete world.

The Temple had been built as a focus for religious devotion and national unity but over time it ceased to be a witness to what could be and, in the eyes of many, particularly the poor, had become a centre of political, economic, and religious power. The Temple that was destroyed by the Romans in AD 70 was the third temple to be built or rebuilt on the same site. It was a notable building. Yet it was destroyed. We live in a time when many of the 'temples' or structures of our world seem to be crumbling. As we seek a new way forward, the message of new possibilities inherent in the way pioneered and gifted to humanity through the way of Jesus suggest guidelines toward new ways of living and the building of communities more suited to human flourishing. If Jesus were to be thought of as a new possibility, a new and continuing focus of divine creativity, an expression of what life could become, rather than in the somewhat static and dogmatic words of creedal Christianity, the church, might have a healing word to share with an ailing and searching society.

The second of the linked images that took hold of my imagination is the suggestion in verses 2 and 3 of our passage that through his ministry and teaching Jesus was charting a new pathway through life's puzzles. In his commentary on Mark, Herman Waetjen wrote, 'The Gospel According to Mark tells the story of the construction of "the way". It features the extraordinary career of Jesus the Jew from Nazareth of Galilee whose unparalleled activity establishes once and for all a new road into life.' In verse 2, Mark recalls words from the Hebrew Bible that conjure up visions of a new pathway being built through life's rough wilderness times and places. Mark's first readers would have thought of the words of Second Isaiah (Isaiah 40:3) about a voice crying out in the wilderness and calling for the preparation of the way of the Lord, building a new and straight highway on which God might lead his people into newness. Life for Jesus followers after the fall of the temple had become desert-like and they yearned for a new pathway, through life. The old maps no longer worked; a new map was needed. Mark's conviction, underlying his Gospel, is that Jesus represents a new pathway on which humanity may walk hopefully into an uncertain future.

According to Acts 9:2, the first Christians were called 'followers of the way'. Implicit in the title is that Christians understood themselves to be part of a movement, a journey, and a pilgrimage on the pathway pioneered by Jesus. It was only later that they came to understand themselves as members of an organisation, servants of static structures and guardians of imposed beliefs. I like the image of Christianity as 'the Way'. It conjures up ideas of adventure, journey, exploration, risks taken and fresh pathways discovered. It suggests a more dynamic understanding of Christian living than being primarily members of a structured organisation. Mark describes the ministry of Jesus as a journey, hurrying on towards the next challenge, the next opportunity to weave healing, forgiveness and generosity into individual and communal living, ever exploring new ways to serve the possibilities of love in a wilderness world. Mark tells us that Jesus' teaching was given 'on the way', and his disciples discussed the meaning of Jesus' life while they were 'on the way'. The best theology is still done 'on the way'. Jesus may have appreciated the work of John the Baptiser but he returned to Galilee for the pathway of radical love had to be constructed 'on the way', with and for village folk.

In an important but forgotten book, *Recovery of the Protestant Adventure*, Neil Hamilton described how, in American Protestantism, Jesus became domesticated, was reshaped as a servant of the powerful, and was shorn of the challenge inherent in the way he pioneered. Hamilton suggests that a re-immersion in the Gospel of Mark might lead to a rediscovery of the sense of adventure at the heart of the Jesus way. The same insight applies to Christianity in New Zealand and Australia. One of the reasons I identify with the progressive movement in theology is that it represents the best opportunity I know of to rediscover the sense of intellectual, spiritual and prophetic adventure that is inherent in 'The Way' we learned from Jesus.

A third interesting image in our reading is found in verse 10: 'Just as Jesus was coming out of the water he saw the heavens torn apart and the spirit descending like a dove on him'. The Greek words for 'torn apart' signify a violent action, a ripping apart of a structure that was thought to be permanent and impossible to dismantle. The image conjures up a dramatically expressed conviction about the love and energy of God flooding the universe, finding a home in every corner of creation and in the deepest places within human lives, luring every person and every part of creation into a future shaped by qualities seen most clearly in Jesus the Spirit-bearer.

The implication is that the presence and energy of God cannot be captured by any temple, structure or dogmatic statement. The spirit blows freely and unpredictably through life. I've been rereading some of the essays of Teilhard de Chardin, a Jesuit scientist and theologian who died in 1955. At the heart of his thinking and praying is an intense awareness of the presence of God in all reality. His views were regarded as being heretical by the Vatican, he was banished to China and his books were not published till after his death. His views are consistent with Mark's image of the heavens being ripped apart enabling the universe to be flooded by Divine love. The image of God as creative and loving energy at the heart of life rather than as a distant and lordly figure has become one of the most helpful insights of modern theology. We cannot whistle up the presence of God as though God were like a doggy on a string but we can grow in sensitivity to the presence of divine energy and love within all of life and in every person. The spirit is present in those of other faiths, in those we cannot understand, among believers and unbelievers, in the lives of both the virtuous and the erring. The heavens are ripped apart and God is emptied into creation and into the human family.

We live in different circumstances than those that shaped the lives of Mark's first readers and hearers. Yet the continuing relevance of Mark's good news remains a lively option for those who, like us, live in a time when the temples, social and economic structures and church systems we've inherited and once depended on are crumbling and in need of radical repair. Mark's three images of Jesus as new creation, builder of life's pathway and symbol of God's presence in a universe shot through with divine energy and love suggest perspectives from which we may contribute to the rebuilding of our world and of the Christian presence within that world. What do you think?

Exploring Further

The commentary by Herman Waetjen is *A Reordering of Power, A socio-political reading of Mark's Gospel*, (1989).

2

Sabbath discipline and the maintenance of identity

Mark 2:23 to 3:6

> Early Christians gathered for prayer and companionship on Sunday, the first day of the week. Others went about their business on the day but this habit was distinctive of the followers of the Way. Centuries later, justification for this custom – now imposed on all citizens of whatever conviction – was written into legislation. It lost any meaning – it became an unwanted imposition.

The seventh day of every week, the Sabbath, a day of rest and renewal in God and in community is, for the Jewish people, a gift to be treasured. It is often said that without the Sabbath the Jewish people might not have survived through all the struggles of a difficult history: 'It's not that the Jews keep the Sabbath, it's the Sabbath that keeps the Jews'. The Christian church has never been sure how to understand, receive or modify this disciplined reminder of the presence and liberating energy of God-love in a wayward world.

Sabbath discipline and the maintenance of identity Mark 2:23 to 3:6

It seems to me there is wisdom in the Sabbath tradition that should not be lightly set aside by those seeking to build a humane, hopeful and generous society. The traditional church interpretation of today's Gospel reading has typically seen it as a graphic illustration of how foolish Jews of Jesus' day had become, lost in a sea of archaic and silly Sabbath rules that obscured life's joy and love for needy neighbours. As Christian and Jewish scholars have worked together in recent decades seeking an understanding of first-century Palestinian Judaism, it has become clear that interpretations like this represent not only an inaccurate understanding of first-century Jewish spirituality and theology but, even worse, has helped to fuel the sinister and death-dealing, anti-Semitic persecution across the centuries that cast such a dreadful shadow over European history.

Jesus was a faithful Jew of his time and he debated strongly with his contemporaries how the ancient Sabbath laws were to be interpreted in the light of God-love. The very fact that Jesus was willing to engage in discussion of how to follow the inherited commandments shows that he cared deeply about them. According to Matthew, he did not envisage any part of the Jewish way being abolished even though he argued strongly that one must look behind the words to the Divine intention that prompted the words in the first place. He was anxious that any rules serve life rather than death. Jesus attended synagogue and he observed the great festivals like Passover. It is unlikely he ever envisaged a future for his followers outside of the Jewish tradition. As a Jewish teacher he engaged in vigorous debate with other teachers of his day about how the Law of Moses was to be understood and lived in first-century Palestine. Jesus had a view and he argued for it.

The Sabbath became particularly important to the Palestinian Jewish community from about 200 years before the time of Jesus. These were years when the Jewish community existed under the strong military and economic might of first the Greek and then the Roman Empires. It was important that they preserve their identity, that they nourish and maintain their deep-down hopes and that they gain strength to withstand the tempting but faith-denying ways of Greek and Roman overlords.

On the Sabbath, two society-shaping traditions were recalled and celebrated. The ancient story was recalled that God rested from creation's work on the seventh day and they too would rest from life's labour, trusting God to run the show without their help. Secondly, the Sabbath was a day to recall how their ancestors were once slaves in Egypt and that God-love had saved them from the economic and social power of the Pharaoh setting them free to create a new society.

Jesus lived within this Sabbath understanding of life and we may recall that at his important sermon at Nazareth (Luke 4:16ff), he drew upon Sabbath imagery as he welcomed the coming of a time when the poor will be embraced by good news, captives will be released, the blind will see and whoever is oppressed will be gifted freedom. In a time of Roman repression, keeping Sabbath was a way of maintaining identity, hope and courage in difficult times. It was also a way of declaring that, though they might be shaped by Roman expectations for six days, on the seventh they would live according to the rhythms of their own identity.

Today's Gospel catches Jesus engaging in debate with other teachers as to how best to live within Sabbath possibility. He represents a more liberal interpretation of Sabbath obedience, a view that was supported by the villagers among whom he ministered, but brought him into spirited debate with those who followed a more restrictive understanding of Sabbath behaviour. Those who have engaged in debate with other Christians about how Christians should live in the presence of gay persons will know just how intense and unsettling religious debate can become. The underlying issue, in both first-century Jewish debate and twenty-first century Christian debate has to do with differences as to how best Jewish or Christian identity is to be maintained within the ongoing issues and structures of human living.

Sabbath discipline and the maintenance of identity Mark 2:23 to 3:6

As to the matter of healing on a Sabbath, no first-century Jew would have argued for a rule that forbade work if a life were to be saved. There were, however, arguments as to what constituted work on Sabbath. The saying of Jesus that Sabbath was made for humanity and not humanity for Sabbath is typical of Jewish teaching that 'The Sabbath is given to you; you are not to be delivered to the Sabbath'. The Christian stereotype that the rabbis were, and have continued to be, a bunch of dour, sour scholars imposing narrowly legalistic boundaries on human living is simply not true of mainstream Judaism. Sabbath was a day of great joy. A tradition developed that the arrival of Sabbath on Friday evening at sunset was greeted as though one were welcoming a much-loved queen or bride.

In 2008, Kathleen and I attended such a service at a hall being used as a synagogue in Jerusalem. We sat in different places with a screen hiding men and women from each other, as is the custom in orthodox but not in progressive Jewish synagogues. It was the men's side that had all the fun! The mood was vibrant. The door was open so as not to impede the coming of Shabbat. We sang Hebrew songs welcoming the coming of Shabbat, the bride for whose coming we yearned. We danced around the space as we sang. I was caught up in the sheer drama of the moment. As the sun set and darkness descended, we gave thanks for the coming of Shabbat and for the promise of a new future for all humanity. Later we joined together in a sumptuous feast – perhaps symbolising the feast of the reconciled human community of which we dream. Twenty-four hours later, on Saturday evening, we were part of a group who, in a home setting, farewelled Shabbat in the service of Havilah. The mood was more solemn. A Sabbath devoted to worship, learning, thoughtful reflection in the company of family and friends was over. Candles lit at Shabbat's coming the previous evening were extinguished; spicy food was eaten with a prayer that the spicy taste of Shabbat would continue through the coming week. Our host reminded us how each Shabbat was experienced as a foretaste of the world to come, of creation's promise fulfilled. Now we must wait for another week anticipating the return of Shabbat.

During the same day, our group experienced another side of the day that brought us and our hosts to shared and thoughtful laughter. We met for discussion in a basement room under another synagogue. The rooms were in darkness. One of our hosts asked if one of the Christians would please turn the lights on as such an action would be regarded as work done on the Sabbath if performed by an Orthodox Jew. We all saw the funny side of our predicament and laughed at how Jews and Gentiles need each other!

Early Christian groups, who initially observed Shabbat, eventually ceased to observe this distinctive Jewish ritual, as an increasing number of Gentiles – owing no allegiance to Jewish custom – identified with the Jesus Way. Instead, they gathered on the first day of the week to recall the resurrection of Jesus and their hopes for a future shaped by resurrection values. As a token of the future they hoped for, they shared a simple meal of bread and wine, food of the poor, as recognition of the sharing society they dreamed of and worked for. They welcomed Jesus to be present with them in their simple meal just as Jews welcomed Shabbat as a reminder of their identity in God, their hopes for a new society and the recognition of ever present God-love.

Over the centuries, as Christians sought to enact Sabbath legislation on Sunday, they sadly lapsed into the sort of legalism they criticised the Jews for. During the 17th century, Puritans in England and Scotland forbade sport and other forms of human relaxation on Sundays. The sense of Sabbath joy was lost and a somewhat legalistic and fun denying set of well-policed rules was set in place. I recall in younger days observing strange arguments as to what was and was not permitted on Sunday. In 1959, I taught in a boys boarding school. The principal reluctantly agreed that on Sunday it was permissible to hit a tennis ball against a volley board but that it was forbidden to hit the ball across the net to another player and to keep score!

It's easy to smile at antiquated Sunday rules that reflected a type of spiritual hair-splitting but the question remains whether we might not have thrown out a precious baby with the dirty bathwater when the Christian community – out of fear of legalism – gave away precious insights into Sabbath existence. It's right that we no longer try to impose our Sabbath restrictions on to other people but there may be disciplines we as a Christian community have lost as reminders of who we are, what we hope for and of the presence of God-love surrounding and encouraging us.

I've learnt a great deal from Muslim friends over the years particularly regarding their observance of the season of Ramadan. A statement on Ramadan prepared for the NZ Muslim community describes it as a time when community is built, life in God-love is encouraged and the stories of their tradition are re-embraced. I recall sharing an Itfar, or fast-breaking evening meal, during Ramadan at the Otahuhu mosque. There were hundreds present for a sit down meal following sunset and evening prayers. This happened each evening for the six weeks of Ramadan, all catered for by families who took upon themselves the cost of catering and cooking. During Ramadan, the complete Qur'an was recited and money was given for the relief of the poor and the sick were visited. It's an expression of the same impulse that lies behind the biblical Sabbath.

Have we lost something? The underlying question behind Sabbath (or Ramadan) observance might be stated as: how can we remain truly human, and, for us, consistent with the Jesus Way in a world hell bent on environmental destruction, nationalistic posturing and a global economic system promoting greed as though it is a virtue? In a world like that, how will we maintain our essential identity as followers of the servant way pioneered by Jesus, as people who having glimpsed fragments of what the future could be, reach out in prayer toward a future shaped by justice, peace and generosity? We welcome such a future, even fragments of it, as a gift to be welcomed and lived into. Have we lost something? I don't know the detailed answer but I think I know the question. Perhaps we could explore new ways of using Sunday morning. What do you think?

Exploring Further

Abraham Joshua Heshel, *The Sabbath* (1951) is a great place to begin a rediscovery of Sabbath rhythms. Walter Brueggemann, *Sabbath as Resistance: saying No to the culture of now* (2014) represents a contemporary and socially sensitive re-discovery of sabbath.

3

Naming Jesus and doing Jesus

Mark 8:27-38

> Before Jesus became a doctrine to be believed, he represented a way of living, a deeper sensitivity to our neighbour and a hope for a future where everyone had a secure place within the human community. We may have the most sophisticated theology of who Jesus was and is but unless those clever words lead to an ever fresh 'doing' of Jesus, they fail at the first hurdle. Jesus said: 'Not everyone who says to me, "Lord, Lord", will enter the Kingdom of heaven, but only those who do the will of my father in heaven.' (Matthew 7:21.)

There's no shortage of advice as to how the Western Church can so reform its life that its future will be assured. I share some of the anxiety that's about but deep down I'm more interested in the future of the Jesus movement than I am in the immediate future of inherited denominational structures. That's not to say I don't care about church structures. The Gospel needs some sort of embodiment of the way pioneered by Jesus and bequeathed to humanity. It's the way denominational structures simply reflect current business models rather than gospel priorities and values that troubles me. The deeper question for the church, in good times and in bad, is how do we view Jesus and how can we allow the way of life he pioneered to shape our living, our believing and our ways of being church? Church structures and denominational forms come and go but this foundational question persists: Who is Jesus and how do we follow him? The life and usefulness of the church stands or falls on how we 'name Jesus' and how we 'do Jesus' in the time and place where we live.

Our Gospel reading for today presents us with a first-century attempt to name Jesus and to identify the way of life he bequeathed to humanity. This story, set in the villages of Caesarea Philippi, north of the Sea of Galilee, may be the record of a historical event but I suspect the story is best read as a parable that reshapes a remembered incident from the ministry of Jesus. The story certainly reads like a parable. Mark's version of the Jesus story grew from the life of small groups of Jesus followers who lived in the area that is now Southern Syria, among 'the villages of Caesarea Philippi'. Discussions about the identity of Jesus, his significance within the larger story of God's dealings with humanity and what it might mean for them to follow his way in turbulent and uncertain times, would have been common in their house churches.

Mark was written about the year 70AD soon after the destruction of the Temple in Jerusalem by the Roman army following years of bitter warfare between Jewish nationalists and Roman colonisers. Christian refugees fleeing from the turmoil and suffering in Jerusalem made their way north and settled among the villages of Caesarea Philippi. It soon became clear that their naming of Jesus differed from the views espoused by the non-Jewish villagers among whom they found a new home.

Today's reading describes a conversation that could have taken place in one of the house churches of Caesarea Philippi many years after Jesus left his disciples. Mark imagines the conversation taking place in the presence of Jesus and during his ministry. He pictures Jesus gathering his disciples and asking them who and what they believe he represents within the purposes of God. Later conversations in Caesarea Philippi are read back into the ministry of Jesus. It was well known that Jesus had identified with the renewal movement led by John the Baptiser and some understood his ministry as a continuation and amplification of the work of John. It's a view likely to have been held by villagers of Caesarea Philippi who suffered from the Roman presence and yearned for the day when the land would be shaped by justice and village-style hospitality. Another suggests Jesus was Elijah who some believed would come before 'the great and terrible day of the Lord'. Others place Jesus within the long and honoured tradition of prophets who called the nation back to the dream that led Moses in search of a society shaped by fairness and peace.

The fourth contributor is Peter, remembered in the villages of Caesarea Philippi as a noted leader in the early church in Jerusalem. Reflecting his Jewish inheritance Peter declares that Jesus is the Messiah, the long awaited representative of God whose coming would fulfil all the best dreams and aspirations of Israel. The first followers of Jesus were Jews – Christian Jews that is. They attended the Temple, they knew the ancient scriptures of their people and, as well, on the first day of the week, they met for a simple meal and recalled the teaching and deeds of Jesus the Jew. He was for them the fulfilment of all that was best in the tradition they loved. It was inevitable they would name him as Messiah. But this was a description that held little meaning for the non-Jews in Caesarea Philippi.

In Mark's parable of the naming of Jesus, Peter's choice of 'Messiah' is not so much rejected as waved aside. Mark seems to be more interested in how to follow or 'do the Jesus way' than in accurately naming Jesus. Perhaps it's still more important to 'do' Jesus than to 'name' Jesus. According to Mark, doing the Jesus way means to set out on a pathway of servant living, setting aside personal comfort in the service of good news that the God-Kingdom, the world as God intends it to be, is a possibility. The term Messiah may have been a respected term in Jewish circles but Mark, according to this parable, is hesitant about naming Jesus as Messiah. Herman Waetjen spells out the reason in his commentary: 'The Messiah or Christ title... is essentially elitist... It denotes a King who is seated at the pinnacle of the socioeconomic pyramid over which he rules. To perpetuate his reign he maintains an army, collects taxes, and supports a temple that is serviced by a priesthood committed to the preservation of the divine order of his rule... the structures of the society that he governs are vertical and therefore, because they foster oppression and dispossession, are dehumanizing.'

It's clear from the rest of Mark's Gospel that the God-rule Jesus is establishing is a new moral order built on the dignity of every person and the search for good human community. Mark is clear that if Peter's contribution is to be retained, it must be filled with new content. It's worth noting that throughout his telling of the Jesus story, Mark gives Peter and his fellow disciples a hard time. They are pictured as consistently misunderstanding, even opposing, what Jesus is trying to do and finally denying and deserting him in his time of greatest need. It's Mark's way of reminding the churches of Caesarea Philippi that the Jerusalem leaders didn't always get it right. They needed a more open, inclusive and courageous form of Jesus-following than that modelled by the named leaders of the early church. The church needed a more expansive understanding of Jesus than was encapsulated in the title Messiah.

As I read into the second half of our reading, I sense a shift from academic debate about the naming of Jesus to an emphasis on what it means to 'do the Jesus way'. This is surely an important clue for the church in our day. Is it possible to set aside the arid and divisive debates that have so marred the life of the church in recent decades and instead ask how together we can learn to 'do the Jesus way', take the risks involved, bear the cost of what we're called to be and do and contribute to the healing of the world? Should this become the dominant question attended to by church assemblies, parish councils and presbyteries? Could we replace reports on church buildings, national budgets and declining numbers with conversation about what it might mean to 'do Jesus' in a secularised world.

Note how Mark quietly drops the term Messiah and instead describes Jesus as 'Son of Man'. According to Mark, this is the favoured title of the historical Jesus. It seems that Jesus saw himself as the new human being, the embodiment of God's non- violent nature. Jesus is portrayed as the true human being who, in the midst of struggle – even in the presence of death – remains faithful to the non-violent God. How differently human history would have developed if from the beginning Jesus had been understood as the new possibility for human living, the human being par excellence, Son of Man and brother of all humanity. For a start, we would have been spared the destructive debates between Christians and Jews as to whether Jesus was the Messiah who in claiming this status also swept aside the dignity and respect that belonged to the Jewish people.

Let's now return to our time. Imagine a meeting convened to see if we can agree on a title that might best describe Jesus and the style of life he promotes in the 21st century. Some see him as a judge, setting moral boundaries and keeping so called 'sinners' at a safe distance. They create a judgmental Jesus. Some African Christians describe Jesus as the Great Ancestor, the one from whom a stream of living water still flows and in which we can bathe and be invigorated. The poor of many lands describe him as the Liberator whose memory and presence energises and guides them toward a future where no one is left out and where everyone has food and shelter, friendship and encouragement. Christians who stood against the great tyrannies of our time, apartheid South

Africa, Nazi Germany, and Stalinist Russia are in no doubt who Jesus is. He's the Lord and in his name they will march to no other tune than the one they learn from the Gospels. For others, shaped by an evolutionary world-view, Jesus is the man from God's tomorrow, the one who embodies what life can become.

The discussion goes on for, in the end, Jesus fits no formula. There will never be agreement as to how Jesus should be named. We'll always name him according to the need and the challenges we face. What does continue is the invitation to 'do Jesus', to so live that his renewing energy is set free in our ailing world. The future of the church, of the Christian adventure and, I think, of humanity, requires that there will always be a people in whom the way of Jesus is growing and who by whatever name they call him continue to build the road for which he laid the foundations.

Exploring Further

Two commentaries on Mark, written with a helpful awareness of our times and the social and political realities of first-century Palestine, are: Ched Myers, *Binding the strong man: a political reading of Mark's story of Jesus* (1992) and Herman Waetjen *A Reordering of Power: a socio-political reading of Mark's Gospel* (2014).

4

For which all else is expendable
Mark 9:42-50; Luke 4:14-21

> In this sermon, I explored a difficult to appreciate Gospel text – the sort of text we might skip over as representing first-century imagery that no longer speaks to us. They're not words to be heeded literally but the metaphorical meaning persists across the centuries. Is there a pearl of great value for which one might give up socially approved ambitions? Is there a gentle summons that takes precedence over all else?

I want to take you on a long detour before we get to the lectionary Gospel reading in Luke 4. I begin with the strange words of the Mark 9 reading. The language and imagery is stark and unusual. Those who do harm to 'the little ones' – the marginalised, the vulnerable, the needy – are warned they are fit only to be weighted by a concrete collar and tossed into the sea. If they want to qualify for life within the God-kingdom they must be willing to amputate hands and feet, even pluck out an eye as signs they seek to be free of wrongdoing. My first impulse over the years has been to set this reading aside as an example of outmoded thinking. But I now think these strange and exaggerated sentiments carry important meaning for those wanting to live within the Way of Jesus.

Clearly, the words are not to be taken literally. They reflect the cruel and vindictive type of tribal law that still persists in some parts of the world. Islamic State leaders have sought to impose a dreadfully harsh misrepresentation of eighth century desert punishments and there are 'Christians' who live on the same violent page. Theft is punished by the amputation of a hand, escape from slavery by the amputation of a foot and sexual misconduct by the removal of an eye. Some scholars suggest that this primitive practice might have originally represented a somewhat progressive and humane form of punishment in an era when death was regarded as normal punishment for even the smallest of crimes against the community. A notable early church theologian, Origen, pondered on our passage and having decided that his greatest temptations were to come through his sexual organs rather than hands or feet, castrated himself with a clam shell and lived as 'eunuch for the sake of the Kingdom'. Why did Mark include such forceful, extravagant and easily misunderstood language as part of his record of the enduring message of Jesus?

It seems to me that behind the graphic and violent language of today's reading is a question that goes to the heart of life and its possibilities: Is there anything in life, any cause, any truth, any insight or value that is more important than our own comfort and the comfort of those we love? Is there any cause or possibility that might oblige us to break ranks and challenge what others regard as proper and godly behaviour? Is there any cause or activity that we should allow to disrupt our plans and ambitions? In the imagery of our text, is there anything in life more important than our sight, our mobility and the use of our hands? Jesus, it seems to me, lived from within a solid 'yes' to these questions. So what is this 'ultimate

For which all else is expendable Mark 9:42-50; Luke 4:14-21

concern', this possibility that claims precedence over all that is commonly regarded as being essential to the good life?

It can't be Christianity, Islam, Hinduism, Judaism or any of the great religious traditions. Each began as a movement of spirit and each was born from a desire to be servant of peace and harmony but sadly each has contributed more than their share of grief to the human family. None of them has remained consistently faithful to the original peace-seeking impulses that brought them into being. Each religion points beyond itself to something deeper and more elemental in life. So perhaps it's 'God' that's more important than anything else we can imagine. But, which 'god', which understanding or image of the deity? Is it Allah or Yahweh, God the Father, or Brahmin, God the all-powerful who creates in one powerful act or God the cosmic lover who in weakness identifies with human weakness and fragility? Disagreement over the meaning of 'God' as variously understood within the human family has too often been a cause of strife, even of violent persecution of those whose understanding of 'god' differs from those who have power.

We need to go deeper in our search for what is ultimately important and takes precedence over all else. The word 'God' has become overgrown with religious politics so we need to reach for the 'god beyond god'- the unnamed impulse, the voice, the call, the event, the invitation embedded in the deeper places of life and present in everyone. Frequently obscured by the counter claims of a greedy, indulgent and self-serving society, this weak and gentle voice continues to nudge and invite from the deep places of human existence. It's like a whispered invitation to find one's true life in a never-ending search for justice and peace, generosity and hospitality in a sadly divided and frequently violent world. It's like a call from beyond yet also from within, emerging from humanity's past yet directing us toward future possibility. In some religious traditions it's described as 'Spirit', a mysterious and silent, wind-like presence, a whisper that persists.

John Caputo, a contemporary theologian/philosopher of uncommon insight, suggests that we should be less concerned about God's 'existence' than about God's 'insistence'. He refuses to attach the word 'God' to this deep down call lest he inadvertently create a word picture that itself becomes a matter of debate or is freshly captured by creeds and systems that tend to dull human sensitivity to this insistence deep within, this invitation to share in the building of a healed world, a world where justice, peace, generosity and hospitality are embedded in the structures of life. We may have to set aside all we have been taught about God if we are to hear this insistent call to world building. It's a voice that cannot be contained within human cleverness – it's like a summons that emerges from the silence beyond our words.

In the Christian tradition, the name 'God' is the nickname we have given to this insistent voice, this event, this happening, this questioning of the taken for granted, that pesters us and invites us to live within a shared search for peace, justice, hospitality and generosity. The word 'God' does not refer to a person-like being but to a summons, a presence luring us to go in search of whatever brings healing to our fractured and troubled world. The words and deeds of Jesus represent a response, within first-century conditions, to this call deep within that takes precedence over all else, the ultimate concern around which the whole of life can be shaped. Jesus lived toward a dream he described as the God-Kingdom – a kingdom where 'the little ones' are taken seriously and the human world is being rebuilt around their needs. This surely is the movement and summons at the heart of life that takes precedence over every other claim for our attention.

The language of 'amputation' in our text seems appropriate to what I've suggested. To say 'yes', however hesitantly, to the call sensed in the depths of life inevitably means saying 'no' to other voices that clamour for our attention – the taken for granted values and societal ambitions that surround us like water surrounds a fish. In western middle class culture, the expectation is that we will

For which all else is expendable Mark 9:42-50; Luke 4:14-21

each seek after power, prestige and possessions as the driver of our living and the measure of our success. So deeply embedded are these values in the western psyche that to set them aside is like a form of amputation. We could rephrase the text: 'If you seek to be a servant after the manner of Jesus you will need to cut off the search for power lest in gaining the world you lose your soul. If in your search for possessions you find yourself growing rich while others are in need it is better that you cut off the greedy impulse lest you become a toxic intrusion within the human family. If in your search for prestige and position, you find yourself to be walking over the rights and aspirations of others, it is better to cut off these attitudes and discover the true meaning of simplicity lest you become a harmer rather than a healer within the human community.'

A few years ago, two young Kiwi couples associated with an Auckland church holidayed in Myanmar. They were drawn there by a sense of adventure and by the needs of this damaged nation. They were overwhelmed by human need and encouraged by the resilience of ordinary people in the face of hardship and deprivation. Many were hindered from a fuller use of their best gifts because they lacked access to small amounts of capital that might enable them to set up a modest, village-based business. A man asked the group: 'Can you help us?' Two of them were law graduates, one a doctor and the fourth an economist. They discussed how they might respond to what they had experienced in Myanmar. Their initial response was to say: 'This is a worthy project for someone else, perhaps for a government department or an international aid agency. Why us, who have so many other things to do with our lives?' Then one of the group added a new question: 'Why not us?'

The question was a game breaker. Reflecting on the event in 2013 one of the group remarked: 'This is my story of a time when I said "yes" rather than "no". After reflecting on the big social problems faced by our world – disease, war, environmental degradation, the socioeconomic divide and inequality – I think one of the most revolutionary things we can do in this day and age is to take a breath, grit our teeth and speak but one word: ... yes'.

Since then, that initial group have set up and successfully operate a small bank making micro loans to marginalised people unable to gain credit from commercial banks. The work of the organisation they developed is flourishing in Myanmar and has recently extended its work into Malawi. Was it the 'god beyond god' the insistent invitation, the event that disrupts our best laid plans that they heard whispering to them in the words 'why not us?' In saying 'yes' to the insistent voice within, to the invitation to be healers and justice builders, they necessarily had to set aside other ambitions that might have claimed their best gifts. Other possibilities had to be amputated.

In the spirit of today's Gospel reading, we might think of the church as 'a community of the amputated' – made up of people who have heard the whispered call inviting them to participate in the rebuilding of our broken societies and to escape from the clutches of values and systems that contribute to greed, violence and injustice. Sadly, the church across the centuries and into our own time has become compromised and, rather than amputating signs of complicity with what harms life, has in fact been a willing and enthusiastic accomplice, an apologist and a beneficiary of political, economic and social systems that fuel injustice. Perhaps a new church, a new expression of the Jesus way, can be born in our time.

The Gospel reading set down for today includes the words of Jesus in the synagogue at Nazareth when he declared how he intended to respond to the whispered insistence deep within, the voice that would not go away. In his three years of ministry among the villages of Galilee and constantly harassed by guardians of injustice and oppression, he was determined to share good news with the poor, to release captives, give sight to the blind, free the oppressed and live within the ancient dream that God is the energy of love and the possibility of peace. It was a calling that took

For which all else is expendable Mark 9:42-50; Luke 4:14-21

precedence over personal comfort and all the normal trappings of human success.

Exploring Further

In a time when denominational structures and distinctives are crumbling, we need to ask if they represent a pearl of great price for which all else is expendable or if they are historically-conditioned expressions of the Jesus Way that need to be superseded. We're unlikely to grow another arm or leg to keep us going as we are but perhaps we need some amputations that will fit us for a more nimble and appropriate response to the whispered summons to participate in the agenda Jesus identified with when asked to preach at Nazareth (Luke 4:18-19).

About the author

Rev. Dr Keith Rowe is a retired Minister of the Word in the Uniting Church in Australia. Ordained by the Methodist Church in New Zealand, he served for thirty years in New Zealand as Parish Minister, Theological College Lecturer and Principal. He was President of the Methodist Church of New Zealand in 1992-3.

He transferred to the Uniting Church in Australia and served in two Sydney parishes, was chair of the Assembly Doctrine Commission and, for twenty-five years, a contributor to the devotional magazine *With Love to the World*. Kathleen and Keith returned to New Zealand upon retirement and live in Napier, Hawkes Bay.

Keith has degrees in history and in theology from The University of New Zealand, Otago University, Union Theological Seminary (NY) and a doctorate in theology from San Francisco Theological Seminary.

Concerns and interests that have shaped him in both ministry and retirement include interfaith dialogue, seeking social and economic justice, the search for a hospitable and inclusive society, and the ongoing task of exploring the shape of Christian living and believing in a world being reshaped by amazing scientific discovery and technological innovation, yet sadly divided by ancient prejudices and economic and cultural injustice.